WHATEVER NEXT?

BY THE SAME AUTHOR...

Great White Palace. Deerhill Books.

WHATEVER NEXT?

From Biba through Fashion week
and on to buy an English Island.

Tony Porter

Matador
9 Priory Business Park,
Wistow Road, Kibworth Beauchamp,
Leicestershire. LE8 0RX
Tel: 0116 279 2299
Email: books@troubador.co.uk
Web: www.troubador.co.uk/matador
Twitter: @matadorbooks

ISBN 978 1785890 611

British Library Cataloguing in Publication Data.
A catalogue record for this book is available from the British Library.

Printed and bound by CPI Group (UK) Ltd, Croydon, CR0 4YY
Typeset in 11pt Minion Pro by Troubador Publishing Ltd, Leicester, UK

Matador is an imprint of Troubador Publishing Ltd

To B:
Who never ever gives up on anything.

Acknowledgments

Mark and Jane Grimshaw;
for their willing help at all times.

To Alan Jones:
for his skill and patience.

CHAPTER ONE

I hardly ever succeeded in getting my first service in the right box, but this time I did. Reaching out wide, my friend Ian took a great swipe, sending the ball back, high above my head and way over the baseline.

Even as I called "Out!" and "30–15" I saw it bounce once, then over the fence into the long grass on the other side. This called an automatic halt to the game. Those balls were issued by the headmaster of Broadwater Manor House School, and I had signed for a box of six of the best Slazengers, to be returned complete and in good condition.

Dropping my racket, I shouted, "I'll get it!" and went to climb over the fence. Well, not really a fence; more like railings, iron ones, with pointed tops and a horizontal bar running nearly a foot below the top. These particular railings were very rusty, apparently not having been painted for years. This didn't deter me, though, and, scrambling up, I found that each tennis shoe fitted neatly between two of the spikes. Balancing briefly and straightening my knees, I jumped.

My right foot slipped out easily, but the left one, maybe twisted in the action of jumping, became trapped, and as my body fell forwards, one of those wicked rusty spikes stabbed right through my left leg. The only thing I remember about that moment, apart from the pain, was a large amount of blood staining my white shorts as I hung there upside down. Then I passed out.

It would have taken Ian a good five minutes to run to the school, find someone and return, and so, faced with this unconscious body hanging upside down on the railings, he decided to unhook me. In doing so, he tore away the flesh, an act for which he was blamed and reprimanded later on. Poor thing, he was twelve years old and was only trying to help. I didn't hold it against him at all. Either way, I bear a three-cornered scar to this day.

Approaching the age of thirteen and with imminent entry to public school, this injury, and its consequent "off games" for three months, would have been serious for any boy. For me, it was infinitely worse, not to say the last straw. That game of tennis had taken place only a couple of weeks into the summer term of 1947, the first term in the whole of my young life when I had been allowed to play any games at all.

* * *

My mother, Phyllis (Phyl), had had a sheltered life in Rotherham, and when a dashing young solicitor from Teddington on the River Thames whisked her away to the South Coast, she had a great and happy time, but, as we

2

always suspected, she knew little about the "Birds and the Bees". Well, he knew all about them! When I say "he", I am talking about Charles Vernon Porter (CVP), my father, known to everyone except his scary mother as "Jim". (Even he could never tell us why!).

Jim and Phyl Porter

My sister Ann came along very quickly, followed by four more of us. I was the first of those four, born (in a bed pan!) in Hove, Sussex in 1935, with a problem in my insides. It wasn't life-threatening. It had to do with various bits of me that were not in the right places, and had to be moved one by one. The first operation took place when I was three, the last when I was eleven. I remember little about the details, only that in latter years I was under the care of a specialist at Great Ormond Street Hospital for Children who rejoiced in the name of Professor Twistington-Higgins. Until that final operation, I had been banned from all games. Every afternoon, as my friends ran, kicked and tackled, batted and bowled, I was always on my own, gardening in the grounds. To this day, while I am happy to clean up or light a bonfire, I leave the digging, weeding and planting to others!

We grew up in a big Edwardian house in Shoreham-by-Sea, Sussex, called Weppons, named after another house that had belonged to my father's legal mentor elsewhere in the county. It stood on a site at the corner of Ravens Road and Mill Lane, where there was a high brick pillar. This proudly bore a shiny brass plate proclaiming 'C.V. Porter, Commissioner for Oaths'. I never quite understood this plaque for two reasons. Firstly, it was a constant source of irritation for CVP, since it was frequently used as a target by passing kids whenever they felt like throwing stones. Secondly, if, as very occasionally happened, it attracted someone who actually wanted to swear an oath, it invariably occurred just as lunch was put on the table or, worse, as cocktails were being poured. Was it worth the delay and half an hour in his study with his 'client', all for the ten-shilling note, which eventually changed hands? That plate passed to brother David, the youngest and only child to embrace the law. He still has it, out in Uganda, dents and all!

We had a gardener called Green. We called him Mr Green, but to our father in those days it was just plain Green. We thought he was wonderful, mainly because of the potting shed. This is where he would retire at lunchtime, seated on a tall wooden stool to eat his bread and cheese at one of the high benches. Crowding round him, we would not miss a single word of his yarns of long ago, and would watch hopefully as he sliced dark yellow cheddar with his slightly soiled wooden-handled gardener's knife. Occasionally we would strike lucky with a morsel; a tiny taste of cheddar even now conjures up a picture of that lean-to shed, with its earthen floor, pots of every size, the smell of ripe compost and old Mr Green in his flat cap munching away with an occasional slurp of sweet tea from a chipped enamel mug.

I wish we had a garden like that today (as long as we had a Mr Green to help us!). Lots of friends had smart front gardens like us, with neatly edged lawns, stone paths, roses, lavender and any amount of colourful borders. But we had the big back garden as well where the fruit and vegetables grew. Gooseberries, raspberries, loganberries, strawberries were supplied all summer long. The orchard bore us apples (Cox's orange pippins) pears, cherries and peaches. CVP's pride and joy was a single plum tree which gave only about three fruit per year, but they were Victoria plums, and there was always quite a ceremony when he and Mr Green deemed them ripe for picking.

There were large earthenware pots with lids where sea kale thrived in the darkness, and nearby were potatoes, rhubarb, cauliflowers and cabbages. At the bottom of the garden there was a great sandy patch given over to asparagus, which both our parents loved. Early in the season, outside the big double garden gates that opened onto the street, a large lorry would appear with sand, which would be barrowed all day down to the asparagus bed. Months later little pink green tips would appear and, soon afterwards, Phyl would go down with a special fork which cut the precious stuff way down under the sand. When the surplus went to seed, there would grow lush five-foot high ferns, very useful when we wanted to play hide and seek.

There was one special lawn, devoted to a tennis court. I never really saw why. The adults hardly every seemed to play, but CVP seemed to enjoy the eternal battle with the posts on which the net was suspended. However much he hammered long pins into the lawn, they were always pulled over by the weight of the net itself, which was then far too low in the centre to play a proper game. He also loved pushing a contraption that was supposed to make straight white lines on the grass (though they never looked very straight to us!), and forever tried to erect more and more very high netting, to stop stray balls breaking the glass of the greenhouse or cucumber frames. Years later, my brother Nigel and I were to get into serious trouble for playing bicycle polo on that pristine court, using CVP's precious golf clubs as sticks!

We all went to a kindergarten (I have often wondered why we chose to translate the word for a kids' school into German) called Greenfields. Nigel (sixteen months my junior) and I would go together, on the way meeting up with two girls called Lalage and Imogen Mais, who lived in a house called Toad Hall. Their father, S.P.B. Mais, wrote about travel and holidays and I can still remember the smell of his pipe and of all the books in his study. Little did I know that one of the places about which he wrote so poetically and with such huge praise was one day going to be mine! Even the teacher at Greenfields had a link with my future. She was called Miss Pascoe, a good old West Country name.

One Sunday in 1940, CVP took us for one of his favourite walks over the wooden toll bridge at Old Shoreham and on towards the great chapel of Lancing College, the local public school. Halfway along, as we passed Shoreham Airport, we met the headmaster. He and CVP had been chatting for a while when all of us heard the strangest wailing sound coming from the town. The adults stopped talking and hurried back the way they had come; we too turned back, to be told on the way home that we had heard the air raid siren, the first of very many. It was wartime and Hitler had us in his sights.

Seven of us!

There was a door in the hallway of Weppons, which opened onto cold stone steps that led down to an even colder cellar, and a 'shoot' down which the coalman emptied his sacks from the garden above, creating a great mound of coal in one corner. Otherwise there was nothing down there except a pile of blankets and a small kerosene stove.

We were not old enough to be evacuated, so we stayed on at Weppons and hurried down those stairs with our gas masks whenever the siren went at all hours of the day or night. Judy and David were the youngest, and the latter, being only a baby, was privileged to have his very own gas mask into which his whole self was inserted before being zipped up! There was of course breathing apparatus, and we could see his face through a screen, usually screaming in protest!

Down there in the cellar it was cold and frightening. We could hear the drone of the aircraft and the occasional explosion, but as it turned out no houses in our area were seriously damaged. (Much later one was destroyed by a doodlebug. Its ugly engine noise cut out right over our heads, but it glided on a little further before crashing and exploding near Buckingham Road.) On the days that followed raids, we would often find the fins of incendiary bombs and bits of shrapnel. They were duly reported and collected by the police.

"Weppons"

CVP was not called up because his job as a prosecuting solicitor was deemed essential. The law, after all, had to be upheld, war or no war. However, he volunteered for the Royal Observer Corps and, in addition to attending court, spent four-hour shifts (some during the night) on Shoreham beach, identifying incoming aircraft. He would report their type, position and direction of flight to nearby gunners. If they were enemy planes, they would start shooting, guided at night by searchlights as they swept the sky. Occasionally, when he was at home in the evening, he would produce a pack of special cards, which showed silhouettes of aircraft – both ours and German – in black against a white background. There were three angles portrayed: from immediately below, from the side and head on. This last view, considered the most important for obvious reasons, was called the dihedral, and as we tested him mercilessly before supper, we usually showed him just this, without the help of the other two. Eventually we all became fairly adept at telling the difference between, say, a Dornier and a Mosquito!

There were seven of us living in that house, and having a demanding job as vice president of the local Red Cross, Phyl needed some help with the family. This came in the form of Ethel, a middle-aged woman from Cornwall. She was small with thick glasses and a harelip. We all loved her as she got down to running the household in a way with which no one could argue, not even 'The Master' (as she called CVP). He simply didn't know how to deal with Ethel, so mostly thought it best to avoid her. Even this didn't always work. Being very fond of Judy, she always liked to know where the little girl was. One morning, CVP was sitting on the 'throne' reading his *Daily Telegraph*, as was his wont, when there was a knock on the door. "Judy, are you in there?" came Ethel's unmistakably piercing voice. Automatically pursuing his safety policy, he sat tight (no pun intended!), whereupon there came a much louder series of knocks accompanied by "*Judy! Judy!* Are you all right?" Still he didn't move, expecting she would give up and go away. Not a hope! Seriously worried by now about what might be happening to her little darling on the other side of that door, Ethel retreated across the hallway and, taking a medium-sized run, threw her small but pointed shoulder at the bathroom door. It was secured only by a smallish silver bolt, which gave way under the unexpected onslaught. The door flew open and Ethel hurtled through, losing her balance as she came, finishing up lying on the bathmat looking up at CVP. He said nothing, as he turned to the sports page. Although I wasn't there to witness that scene, I can still picture it from CVP's graphic description at the time!

Poor Ethel, it all happened to her. She was in charge of the chickens too and every evening she would go into the garden with a bucket full of grain, banging it with a big wooden spoon. She also uttered a strange chicken-type noise to attract the hens that were free to roam through a large part of the vegetable area. She didn't actually count them as they came running but she made sure they knew it was suppertime. Then, on one occasion, when they were all pecking round her feet, she heard another one, rustling in the hedge. Making her noise and banging her bucket, she went over to shoo this extra bird towards the others. No one was there to see what happened next. The first we knew was when she came slowly through the back door, bucket and spoon in hand, bleeding profusely all over her face, which had apparently been torn by several sharp instruments. Those instruments turned out to be the claws of a sparrowhawk which had been hiding in the hedge, and which objected to this strange face peering at it through the leaves. My mother's first aid skills, which she had learned at Red Cross, had never been so urgently required.

* * *

During those early years, try as I might, I could not avoid trouble. It is hard to remember when it started. Probably at Sunday school in St Nicholas Church, Old Shoreham.

Every week, we were given sixpence each for the collection, which, I confess, was occasionally spent on sweets before or afterwards. But that wasn't the problem. It was the acorns. They were large and intricately carved in ancient wood, standing three feet above both ends of each church pew, and I liked to hang my school cap on them. It was absolutely required, I knew, that I should take it off on entering the church, but there was nowhere to put it, so where better than up on one of those handy acorns? The vicar, other boys' parents and the Sunday school teacher herself all told me not to do it, but I simply could not see what all the fuss was about. In the end, a stern letter from the vicar to my mother ended my habit, but I still could not understand why I had to keep that cap on my knee for nearly an hour each Sunday, when someone had provided such an obvious 'hook' for it.

Whilst on caps and churches, we were taught that, if we saw a funeral procession go by, we should remove our caps out of respect for the dead. I always obeyed this rule, but one day, walking to the bus stop in Worthing, I did it once too often. Spying a hearse waiting at the traffic lights, I doffed my cap, only for one of the undertakers to lower his window, calling out to me: "It's OK, sonny, there ain't no body in 'ere!"

As Nigel and I grew up we did most things together. One day we were in Shoreham doing some shopping for Phyl, when outside the greengrocer I saw, sitting on top of a box full of apples, a particularly large, red shiny one. "Look at that apple!" I said to Nigel, and then, to my eternal shame, "Why don't you get it?" As he hesitated, I urged him on, until, all of

12

a sudden, he seized it, and we both beat it down the street. Well, the shop owner saw what happened, and gave chase. It was Nigel who got caught, Nigel who got clipped round the ear and Nigel who had to hand over the apple. I have wished ever since that I had stepped forward to his aid, but I didn't. He still remembers. Seventy years on, he doesn't go on about it, but in my own head, I will never live it down.

In a way, entirely unintended, Nigel got his own back when we were fooling around one day in the garden. I chased him and he fled into the greenhouse, slamming the door behind him. Maybe it had been raining and maybe the door had swollen, but either way, it jammed and however much he pushed, he couldn't open it to get out. There was nothing on the outside for me to pull, so I went into the house to get something to help open the door. I chose a golf club from the hall and passed it in through a small open window, telling Nigel to hit the inside of the frame of the door with it. Helpless, I stood outside the door to see how he got on. Two blows achieved nothing, so I encouraged him to hit harder. He did, but instead of the frame, he hit the glass, smashing a whole pane. One particularly large jagged piece caught me on the upper lip, causing such a gash that three stitches were necessary in Dr Riddle's surgery. Another lifelong scar!

(That's twice I have mentioned golf clubs, but I do not want to suggest that CVP was in any way a keen player. In fact, he was always saying that he had to give the game up. It wasn't that he lost too many balls, but clubs, which, in exasperation, he was apt to throw deep into the brambles!)

My misfortunes – often my own fault – didn't stop there. CVP had a terrifying mother. Her name was Maud, but he called her 'the Mater'. We had to call her Grandma Porter. She lived in Hove, a dozen miles away, and was chauffeured to our house for lunch every Sunday. She would arrive, with her face caked in white powder all over, except for her lips which were a lurid gash of Post Office red. She liked to arrange herself on the window seat in the lounge, smoking her Du Maurier cigarette and sipping her sherry, to await the appearance of her five grandchildren, in their Sunday best. We dreaded her red and wet sticky kiss, and having suffered it, retired as soon as we could.

There was no special order of appearance, and on one particular Sunday towards the end of the war, quite by mistake, I appeared first. The others followed one by one but, for some reason, Ann was last by some minutes. After an awkward silence, in she suddenly rushed, breathless and flushed with embarrassment. Her complexion radiated health and happiness and her jet black hair shone; perhaps a shampoo was the reason for her late arrival.

Grandma had just lit another cigarette, depositing on it a goodly portion of red lipstick, before laying it in the ashtray as Ann came near. "Oh, my dear," she said, "come here and give me a little kiss. You are so pretty with that black hair of yours; you look just like a little Italian!"

Well, I suppose in a way she did, but we were at war with Italy, and I wasn't going to take this. Striding up, I stood in front of Ann, shielding my beautiful sister who had been so insulted. Without further hesitation, I blurted out at Grandma: "And you look like a German!"

Amidst the deadly hush that followed, the only noise was that of the Mater dropping her packet of cigarettes and lighter into her handbag. With a loud click, she snapped it shut, and swept out of the house, never to return. She died within a couple of months. I can't really remember, but I expect I felt awful.

Soon afterwards the whole family, except Phyl, who stayed behind to cook Sunday lunch, went on one of our longest walks. It took us through Shoreham, over the river Adur to Bungalow Town and right along the beach to a big old fort, which had stood there for ages. It was one of CVP's favourites, but today he was ill at ease, we could tell. He kept looking over his shoulder at a policeman who was following us. As he caught us up, we could see he was senior, with a peaked cap and silver pips on both shoulders. CVP apparently knew him from court and fell back for a chat, while we waited politely, sheltering from the wind behind a giant anti-tank concrete cube (Shoreham beach was one of the most likely points where the feared invasion was expected).

All of a sudden, CVP called me over to join him and the superintendent, as he turned out to be. Immediately covered with guilt, for I knew not what, I obeyed his command.

"Tony, have you been in the garden lately with your airgun?"

"Yes, Daddy."

"And what have you been shooting at?"

"Targets."

"What sort of targets?"

"Targets with bullseyes."

"What else?"

"Nothing."

"What about sparrows?"

I nearly died. How on earth did he know that? And what did the important policeman have to do with it? It was true that just once or twice I had been tempted to lay my sights on a tiny target high in a tree. But not often. I just stood there, my raincoat lashed by the strengthening gale.

"The superintendent says that Mrs de Buriat has seen you from her bedroom window, shooting sparrows. Is that true?"

"Yes, Daddy." *The old cow. I'll never wave back to her again when she's sitting in her window, nor will I pick up a newspaper for her from the shop.*

All three of us were embarrassed, but there was little more to be said. CVP muttered something to the superintendent, who turned back. The family carried on to the fort without me. I sat on the pebbles, half embarrassed, half sulking. Even now, more than a half a century later, the memory makes me cringe when I see a couple of tiny birds swoop down with grace and beauty to pick up some of the grain I have put out for them.

Mind you, CVP wasn't perfect – not quite. He always said that he would not go to church to kneel down and say he had sinned before Heaven and Earth, because he hadn't. Well, except once, he did admit.

To take him round the many magistrates' courts of Sussex, he needed a car. He also needed one to get to the Observer Corps lookout at 2am and home again at 6 in the morning. That wasn't easy though, because there was a severe shortage of petrol. The government supplied him with a small quantity of coupons, which he used to buy petrol in the local garage. However, he had to be very careful how he used the precious fuel, partly because he did not want to run out, and partly because there were conditions attached. One of these said that under no circumstances was he to give lifts.

One morning, early as usual to attend court, he was on his way to Arundel when, a little way ahead, he saw two sailors thumbing a lift. *Not allowed*, he thought to himself, and drove straight past them. Round the corner he came upon two Wrens (female sailors), who were also waving their thumbs in the traditional manner. Without hesitation, as CVP reported to us years later he 'stood on everything', bringing the car to a screeching halt, and took the girls into town. That, he always admitted, was the one time when he actually did commit a sin!

His other admission was that he didn't like foreigners. This sprang from the one and only time when, after the war, he left the precious shores of England to make a one-off appearance in a Parisian court. Before he came home, he set out to find a pair of silk stockings for Phyl. These were like gold dust at the time, and he was thrilled to find a man in the street who agreed to sell him some for a good number of francs. On his return to England he produced them with a flourish, only to be told as tactfully as possible that they were nylons. As far as he was concerned, that was the end of foreigners, and he never ventured forth again. Years later, he was to conceal his disappointment, following the news that I was going out with a Polish girl, but long before I asked her to marry me, he came to love B as much as everyone else, and it became a family joke.

The cocktails that I mentioned earlier were a big part of our parents' lives. Enjoying the twenties and thirties as they had, there were plenty from which to choose, but their favourite by far was a gin and mixed. This consisted of a tot of Booth's Gin, half a tot of French Dry vermouth (or Noilly Prat) and a quarter of a tot of Italian sweet vermouth. No ice, no lemon, no olive and no cherry. This CVP could make expertly and I can still see him inching his way across the lounge, a cocktail glass full to the brim in each hand. He seldom spilt a drop, but if he did, it was deemed a crisis. Lots of scrubbing of the carpet ensued, followed by the inevitable top-up (in the correct proportions of course). The rule was two of these for each of them before dinner (or lunch on Sunday) but almost always it became three because either the potatoes weren't cooked, or the dining room needed heating up a little more!

Once a year they took us all down to Devon to spend a fortnight's holiday at the wonderful Saunton Sands

Hotel. Early on the morning of departure CVP would get up especially early, open the cocktail cabinet and, by a series of the most careful measurements, create a bottle of ready mixed 'Jim Porters', as the cocktails were called by his legal friends throughout the county. After an early breakfast, we would all pile into the Vauxhall (BBP 898) and set off at a stately pace towards the A30. At a certain place around lunchtime, we would slow down and park in a clearing (the same one, of course, every year). Out would come two deck chairs and a picnic table. There was always lemonade for us children to carry off into the woods, but for himself and Phyl, CVP would produce the special bottle and two amazing cocktail glasses made from papier-mâché. With a really long stem, they were black outside with embossed golden dragons climbing up, and inside they were also smooth gold. They would then sit comfortably while they consumed three of the wicked cocktails each, before enjoying a picnic and climbing back into the car. None the worse, we would continue on our way, arriving safely at the hotel in time for dinner!

CVP never drank beer, and only seldom did the two of them have wine (always hock) if visitors came. As he approached his seventy-eighth birthday, he became weak with a blood disorder, and the doctor stopped him drinking. After three months, he became worse, and between us we persuaded the doctor to relent, and the cocktail hour (but only one glass) was reinstated. There was an immediate improvement and he lived happily for three more precious years!

During wartime, it was very difficult to buy sweets of any kind because the makers couldn't get enough sugar, but Phyl discovered a confectioner who lived in Southwick, about three miles east of Shoreham. As a family, we were given coupons for a limited amount of essential foods, including sugar, some of which Phyl saved up. When she had sufficient, she would tell Nigel and me to cycle to the woman's house with the sugar and a little money, asking her to swap them for boiled sweets.

One particular day, we were halfway there when the sirens went, and a policeman told us to get into a shelter quickly, leaving our bikes outside. As we crouched in the semi-darkness, with the other people in there, I remember proudly telling them that our father was on duty on the beach, and it was almost certainly him who had identified and reported the approach of enemy planes. Very impressed they were too, but we pedalled quickly away when the all-clear went and the policeman came in saying, "You can come out now, it was only Spitfires"! We had something to say to CVP when we saw him that evening!

Soon after D-Day, he bought a very large map of Europe, printed on a kind of oilskin fabric. This he hung on the wall in the dining room, and, with help of little flags mounted on pins, kept pace with the advance of the various regiments and the Red Army coming from the east, right up to the fall of Berlin. That and his love of 5,000-piece wooden jigsaw puzzles from a special library in Brighton formed his main evening entertainment at that time.

It was about then that I began to realise that my life was to be marked by mini disasters. As I grew up, they continued unabated, although they were not always my fault, such as the incident of the lounge carpet.

In our house, it was Phyl who made it her job to look after the fires. The stove in the kitchen was always kept going, but the open fire in the lounge was only lit when necessary. Rather than fiddle around with paper, firelighters and matches, she believed in a quicker way. This was to take a shovelful of red-hot coals from the kitchen fire, carry them through the hall, then along the whole length of the lounge, treading carefully on the beautiful dark green carpet which was expertly fitted into every corner. I'll never know why it happened, but one Sunday three or four red coals slid off her shovel and burnt their way right through the carpet before anyone could move them. That was a real crisis and the whole day was ruined. It was only resolved the next morning with the purchase of a big fluffy green rug which remained in the centre of the room until the house was sold soon afterwards. Knowing the ever-honest CVP, he probably pointed it out to the new owners.

On sports day in the summer term at our prep school, many parents attended and there was always a special visitor. All of us boys (including me, although I didn't do sports) would sit on the grass in rows awaiting the VIP. One year the local bishop had been persuaded to preside, and there was a hush as the headmaster took the crackly microphone to introduce him. In due course, the bishop himself stepped forward and started his speech: "Good afternoon everyone, I am—" and the microphone went dead. CVP, who always dragged one foot slightly due to a childhood injury, had arrived a little late. The electric cable lurking in the grass, like some kind of fiendish trap, scored a winner, and ten minutes of embarrassed (especially for me) silence elapsed before the bishop could start again.

Then there was the accident I had with the new Vauxhall Velox (KCD 332). Parking it carefully in the garage, CVP always had to put the radiator almost up to the big bench at the far end, in order to be able to close the doors at the other end behind the car.

These were not locked though, and I was often tempted to sneak inside. There was plenty to see and enjoy. A large vice was fixed to the edge of the bench, and further along, a foot pump, tins of polish, oil, antifreeze and any amount of different tools. When we played hide and seek, the pit was one of the best places to hide. This was a huge deep hole under the car to enable a mechanic to access the underside of the car for repairs and servicing. When not in use, which was most of the time, it was covered with heavy planks for safety reasons. A couple of these could easily be removed, providing a hiding place which, though dark and smelly, could conceal a boy for hours. Not that any of us felt like staying that long.

One day I opened the driver's door of the shiny black car and climbed in. It was fun to turn the wheel pretending to be driving to Worthing or Brighton, and a short beep on the horn made it more realistic. There was no key in the hole – CVP always inserted one before pulling the starter knob – so I saw no harm in giving it a tug myself. To my alarm, as I did so, the whole car leapt forward those vital inches and the silver top of the radiator struck the vice on the bench in front. The car, of course, had been left in gear, but I had no way of understanding such things at that time. I climbed out to find that, although the car, with its handbrake on, had bounced back to its former position, a large dent had appeared in the chrome, seriously spoiling the appearance of CVP's beloved new car.

Not knowing what to do, I retired to one of my favourite haunts, a large cavity behind the huge pile of logs stored in the wood shed. I must have stayed there for a long time, because, when I came out, there was a full-scale hunt for me in progress. Making up some story about how I had been next door, I mingled with the other children, saying nothing about the damage I had wrought.

The next morning it was discovered. CVP had left the house with his full briefcase to attend some court or other, only to return minutes later, telling Phyl what he had found. He had no time to start an investigation and we had to go to school on the bus, but that evening questions flew. We were all asked if we knew anything about it and we all said no, but the next day Phyl put two and two together. She remembered that I had been missing for nearly two hours and then discovered that I had not been next door at all. I cracked under cross-examination and admitted the whole thing.

When CVP came home, the two of them went to the study and we could hear their lowered voices, as we wondered what would happen. When they emerged, CVP announced that I was to be beaten for lying and I was to follow him upstairs to their bedroom. This I did, telling my watching siblings as I went that I wouldn't cry.

I was shattered. My father was the kindest of men and I never thought he would do such a thing, but he did. Well, sort of. When we got to the bedroom, he reached to the top of the wardrobe and produced a long yellow cane. How long it had been there, I had no idea, but he took it in his right hand and told me to bend over a chair by the bed. This I did and he whacked my bum really hard. It hurt a lot and that was enough for me. Without thinking, I stood up, grabbed an alarm clock off his bedside table and flung it at him. It struck him on the shoulder and fell to the floor. I can still see him, as he picked it up, held it to his ear and shook it from side to side.

"You've broken it!" was all he said. It didn't matter much to me though. All I knew was that the onslaught had been interrupted, and I legged it to the door, leaving him shaking the clock in vain. It was clear to the little group, including Phyl, waiting at the bottom of the stairs, that I was not crying, and as I descended, I held my head high, feeling, of all things, something of a hero.

I couldn't guess whether CVP confessed at the time to Phyl that he had failed in his paternal duty, but I did notice a shiny new clock in their bedroom, and years later, it became another family joke.

During the first half of the war, Ann, Nigel and I were sent to Bridlington in Yorkshire for two weeks during the summer holidays. Granny Cross, Phyl's mother, lived there. Her name was Edith and she lived in a flat overlooking the beach. Every year, when we arrived and put down our suitcases, we would enter her parlour to find four or five of her friends having tea. It was quite crowded, and as we found somewhere to sit, a slightly awkward silence would descend until Granny told us to talk. We would ask what she wanted us to talk about, but that didn't matter. They had all come round to hear us talk in our Sussex accent, and as long as we chatted, they were happy. Ann was easily the best, leading the way and posing questions about our school or the journey for us to answer. Now I have come full circle, because I always prick up my ears when, on my travels, I hear the broad accent from the great county of my mother's birth.

Our stays in 'Brid' centred on the sandy beach, but other things that stood out were a trip to Flamborough Head aboard the steamboat *Yorkshireman*, the launching of the lifeboat just opposite Granny's front window, and, of all things, a sweet shop which sold peppermint rock, with BRID written all through its inside. The shop was called Askham, and in huge letters outside, it said: ASKHAM FOR ROCK. We often did!

Around 1944, when Ethel had gone back to Cornwall, Granny Cross moved south to live with us. She was given the room that had been Ethel's, but shared the bathroom with everyone else. It was not an ideal arrangement, as queues formed in the mornings, and CVP found her quite irritating. Before breakfast, he was often quite busy in the dining room, getting ready for court or listening to the BBC Home Service on the radio as he moved his little flags. This required close attention, and he couldn't bear the interruptions as Granny talked about her favourite subjects.

One of these was the 'traffic jimp'. As cars became faster and more powerful, the Ministry of Transport launched a campaign to discourage drivers from speeding and overtaking at dangerous moments. It was called 'Beware the Traffic Jimp', and featured an ugly little creature who, in cartoon form, would sit on the front wing of a car, saying "Come on, come on, overtake, you can make it" as an oncoming vehicle could be seen in the distance. Granny, for some reason, took a liking to the Jimp and collected every example she could, mainly by cutting them out of the newspapers. CVP, a very careful driver, found the little creature silly, and objected when she laid out her latest Jimp cartoons on the family table, while he was attending to his map.

Granny spent hours in her room and told us one day that a German aircraft had flown past her window so close that she had seen the pilot's eyes and he had waved to her. Towards the end of her life, we all returned from an outing to find smoke pouring from the kitchen window. Peering in, we could see Granny by the stove, patiently stirring the contents of a great saucepan, out of which orange flames were leaping towards the ceiling!

* * *

They say behind every successful man there is always the right woman. Our mother, Phyl, was living proof. Quite apart from bearing five children and bringing them up during a world war, when every kind of hurdle was thrown up to make things more difficult, she jumped them all. A good Yorkshire woman, she cooked wholesome food for us. It was never fancy stuff, nor was it always roast beef and Yorkshire pudding, but everything in between as well. We had a larder and meat safe, but no fridge, so regular shopping, complete with ration book, was essential in between her Red Cross duties. She improvised whenever necessary. For instance, ice cream not being available for five years or more, she would make it in the dead of winter by putting a pot of custard in a bucket of ice that she got from the frozen goldfish pond. We loved it, but sadly it wasn't available in summertime!

It was Phyl who made sure the water was hot and the house warm. All the normal things like name tapes and school uniforms were down to her, and she knitted, crocheted or darned without a break in conversation. She loved the garden, good music, Shakespeare, card games and especially being read to by CVP after dinner. (One of her favourites, I remember, was *The Water Gipsies*). She was proud of us and we of her. Between her and all of us there was a special understanding that was to last far into our adulthood. This was especially true of me because, at the age of eight and already having started regular operations, I had contracted scarlet fever; normally this meant that I should have been confined to an isolation ward in a hospital, but she simply moved Ann into our boys' room and put me in hers for ten weeks. Singlehandedly she nursed me back to health without it spreading to any of the others or, indeed, catching it herself! I never forgot what she did for me.

She didn't get us off to school in the mornings. We did that. With no central heating, of course, we would get up on freezing mornings with the most beautiful fern-like patterns etched out of the ice on the inside of the bedroom windows. Dressing as quickly as possible for warmth we would go downstairs to make our own porridge and toast, grab our satchels and gas masks, then run into town for the number 31 bus to Worthing. Nigel and I often had problems there and it was my fault. There were some public toilets a hundred yards away behind the town hall and try as I might, as the time for our bus approached, I nearly always had to run to use them at the last minute. Nigel was infuriated, because I didn't want him to go without me, yet if I was too long and we both missed the bus he didn't see why he should be late for school because of his elder brother. I was really ashamed and eventually overcame the problem, realising it was all in the mind. At the end of each day we caught the same bus back to Shoreham and often had to run home in time to hear 'Dick Barton, Special Agent', which Phyl had always turned on for us at 6.45pm on the wireless.

We had joint headmasters called Nelligan (Nellie) who taught maths and Burton (Bertie) who taught classics and English. Never excelling at maths, I remember failing miserably at algebra exams, and my parents knew it too. One term Nellie coupled a mark of 12% with the comment 'v. poor', and the next term he followed 14% with 'improving'!

As for Bertie, he had a scary temper, but imparted his classics and English knowledge so expertly that it helped me all through public school and well beyond. One thing he could not abide was a split infinitive. Any boy who committed this crime was required to stand on his desk, put both hands on his head and wail at the top of his voice: "Oh no, woe is me, for I have SPLAT an infinitive!" That stopped us, and I teach it to my grandchildren, but alas, most people accept this particular offence these days.

The other thing for which Bertie became especially noted amongst parents was the Broadwater Motto. A terrible Latin pun it was too – 'Per Aqua Latam ad Litus Altius', which being translated literally meant 'Through Broad Water to a Higher Shore'! People would groan, but I have noted that it is still in use today. BMH has its own website, which proclaims it!

Not partaking in sports I was always ready to volunteer for almost anything else and I became something of an actor. I starred in a play called *Brummy Crock* in which the finale was a stirring song (to the tune of 'Hush, Hush, Hush – Here Comes the Bogey Man'), called 'If You Have

British Grit'. It was a roaring success and my loyal parents cheered me to the echo!

As I rose through the school, I became fiercely competitive in class, always wanting to be first to please the father whom I loved and respected so much. This came to a head on Saturday mornings when, in those days, we went to school for half the day. The week's marks were read out at 9.30am, preceded by morning prayers, and it was during this time that I started sweating. Then I would go pale and dizzy, more than once fainting clean out on the floor.

It was ridiculous, and even now, I hesitate to record the fact that it was anxiety for my marks that brought it about. The crazy thing was that I nearly always did well, the only doubt being whether I would come top or second to Ian Sinnott (he of the tennis match). The school and my parents tried everything from firmness to sympathy, but nothing worked. It plagued me, even when I became head boy, till I left and went on to public school. There I boarded and had many other things to take my mind off little matters like marks.

Chapter Two

Boy, what a shock it was, that first term at Radley. My new trunk and full tuck box having been sent 'luggage in advance', I was duly seen off by Phyl on the school train from Paddington with two or three hundred other boys of all ages. I knew not a single one, and with no prospect of seeing my parents for six weeks (gone were the days of being head boy and home every evening), I would have suffered seriously from homesickness, except there was no time for that!

As a lowly new boy, I was allocated a 'Horsebox', a five-foot-square partitioned area with a desk and a small cupboard. There were about twenty of these arranged against two of the walls of 'Social Hall' (houses are called Socials at Radley), which was a large room where boys spent all waking hours for their first four terms, before graduating to having their own study. There were eight Socials, each one having its own Hall. This was where we did our prep in the evenings and spent any little spare time we were allowed.

It was not a friendly or welcoming place. The walls were painted in a creamy colour, which had darkened badly over umpteen years. All the woodwork was a dirty brown, including the boarded floor, and very little light penetrated the tiny old stone windows. There was a hierarchy, within which boys from preceding terms were each trying to establish their importance, and we, the new boys, were subjected to initiation tests, accompanied by worse treatment.

First of all, we were all issued with a small white book (for some reason called the *Grey Book*). This contained a massive amount of information about the college and its rules, all of which had to be committed to memory in two short weeks. We had to learn about the places where only school prefects (called 'Pups'!) were allowed to walk. There was one wide area by the clock tower, for instance, reserved for them. Alongside it there was a narrow path behind a low wall, through which the other four hundred odd boys had to cram, often at the run. We had to learn the names of every Social tutor, the letter allocated to his Social (ours was F) together with each set of Social Colours (F was red and gold).

Then there were the names of the senior prefect and all the other school prefects, any one of whom could recommend that you were beaten for the smallest offence, for instance being found out of the immediate confines of your Social during evening prep time (this happened to me once when I had only gone to work on a problem with a friend who was in my form, but a different Social). Then there was a long list of place names, such as Jackdaw Clump, the Octagons, Covered Passage. All this information had to be assimilated in addition to finding out which don (master) taught which boys in which classroom in which subject at which time. Essential information, but so much of it.

All of this was pretty scary, but to make things worse, after a fortnight, as part of the initiation test, several unpleasant traditions had built up. One was that we had to take turns to climb over the twenty partitions between the horseboxes and back again in an impossibly short time. If we failed, which we always did, we were required to go head first into one of the big and smelly old wooden dustbins built into one corner of the room, while lemonade, or some other chosen liquid, was poured down our trouser legs. It was usually cold and always sticky. It sounds harmless now, but was no fun at the time!

Another charming little 'tradition' concerned a row of lavatories. If, as a boy in your first year, you needed to go, the sitting-down sort I mean, you were forbidden to shut the stable-type door. If you did, a prefect would kick it open and take your name. No one ever explained why. There were no bolts on the doors.

CVP had himself been to Radley and had put my name down by telegram on the day I was born. As the time for my going there grew near, he had been able to conduct some research into which Social I should join. He had chosen one, whose tutor was much respected by all. He had run his Social with great success for eight years; with seven of the ascribed fifteen still to go. This would mean that he would span my five years without handing over to a new man halfway through. Such a change could be so disrupting in a boy's life that parents were keen to avoid it if at all possible. Called Tiny (he was pretty big) Southam, this particular man was a great traditionalist and quite rightly turned a blind eye to the age-old practices of Social Hall. He was a fine character who gave me the self-confidence I lacked, never having been able to join in games and other competitive activities until then. I knew very little about the rules of cricket or rugby, but he was keen on rowing and encouraged me to take it up. I thus spent much time on the river, where I showed early promise.

By this time my sister Ann had been boarding for three years at Malvern College, where she was to become head of house. I was especially glad to find her already home when we broke up at the end of that first term, and I arrived back in lovely Sussex for my holidays. She celebrated by taking Nigel and me out to a baker's shop in Shoreham, called Clark's, where she bought us cream buns and milk shakes. To us it was a real treat as we sat there exchanging news about our three different schools.

Blessed were the weeks of that summer, as I revelled more than ever before in the company of my family, away from the school that, except for Tiny, I had already come to dislike so much. I didn't even think about the day when I would have to set off once more to catch the school train. That summer was the first time CVP took us all to the Saunton Sands Hotel in Devon for a fortnight's holiday and Ann fell madly in love with John Jones, who was staying there with his parents, from Manchester. Every evening, the band played and they would smooch together right up to the last waltz.

CVP had bought Phyl a pale blue ball gown for her to wear on the first night. Having dressed in his dinner jacket, he made some excuse to go downstairs before her. In reality it was to tip off the bandleader, so that when she appeared at the top of the stairs he would strike up with 'In Her Sweet Little Alice Blue Gown'. Phyl wasn't prone to blushing, but did that night as she descended the sweeping staircase and applause broke out! Forty years later we too stayed at Saunton Sands, and sat for a while with the manager, explaining why we had come to live in Devon. I couldn't resist telling him the story of the dress, and was touched when we found a bottle of champagne at our table. CVP would have been touched too, considering the amount of money he spent in that hotel over three annual holidays for the whole family! We really loved it there, spending many hours on the beautiful sandy beach beneath the hotel. Often, there was good surf, which we enjoyed all day long in spite of our heavy plywood boards becoming rather waterlogged.

Later that year our parents fell in love with an enormous house at Steyning. Only ten miles away and still within easy reach of CVP's office it had much more space, inside and out, than Weppons. Romantics as they were, and remembering all that had taken place in the old house, they closed the front door for the last time with heavy hearts. Nowhere near as heavy, though, as CVP's when he drove by a month later and the house wasn't there! The 'nice man' who had bought it to 'house his young family' had turned out to be a developer, who wasted no time in arranging complete demolition and the subsequent construction of eight flats.

CVP never went that way again, but years later I did. That day I presented the residents' association of the flats with a photograph and map of the old house where we spent the war and the garden, now concreted over with garages, as it had been. I also gave them a copy of my old black-and-white photograph of Weppons, adding a mini history of the Porter family's time there. I am glad to say that the photograph was subsequently framed and hung in the landing for all to see. That is all the residents will ever know of the original Weppons, except, I was pleased to note, the word itself which lives on in the name of the flats on the corner of Ravens Road and Mill Lane where CVP's brass plaque used to be fixed. His plum tree and asparagus bed, though, are long gone.

The new house was called Little Drove, but it was anything but little. It had so many bedrooms that we could all invite our friends to stay in the holidays. Ann, in particular, liked this and invited her boyfriend John whenever she could. He was always put up on the second floor, while her room was on the first. So was mine, and more than once, if I came out unexpectedly in the early morning, I would see her tiptoeing up the stairs, her finger to her lip, telling me to keep mum! Quite by chance, John attended the boy's school in Malvern, very near hers. They were not allowed to mix with the girls, but Ann used to say it was extraordinary how often they seemed to visit Smith's at the same time as each other! She did have another boyfriend called Colin. He was very smooth, and she did fancy him, but his letters got too soppy and lovey-dovey for her. So much so that she eventually told him that if he sent another written like that, she would send it back unopened (how she would know if she hadn't opened it, we never worked out!). The threat was effective, and the correspondence dried up. Just as well because, five years later, Ann and John were married at Little Drove, and went on to have three fine children.

The second and third terms at college became marginally more tolerable as I was no longer quite at the bottom of the pile. I learnt rugby and how to scull alone on the Thames in a very fragile skiff, which had a sliding seat and was extremely hard to balance. I was no longer in dread of the initiation tests and bullying of the first term. Tiny was fully aware of everything that went on in his Social, and was always available to give advice. I liked and respected him enormously and was thrilled when, before we went on our holidays, he appointed me head of Social Hall for my fourth term, prior to getting my own study. According to custom, this probably meant that I was being groomed for head of Social by the time I left, which automatically would have made me a school prefect as well.

In Radley uniform at Henley, aged 14

My parents were as delighted as I was. Imagine, then, my horror and sadness when, returning to take up my appointment, I was told that Tiny, who had done so much to help me through that first year, had died suddenly on holiday in Cyprus. His successor was one of the teaching staff to whom I had spoken only once.

Talk about chalk and cheese! In place of the stout jovial man who believed in the old traditional ways, I was now faced with this thin, pale person who disagreed with everything for which his predecessor had stood, and set about 'modernising' his new Social from top to bottom.

This bade ill for me, especially when he arrived unexpectedly in Social Hall one day, soon after I had taken up my position as head. I wasn't there but the usual initiations were in progress, with at least one new boy being 'lemonaded' upside down in one of the bins. The man did not hesitate. Ordered to his study, I was summarily dismissed from my position as head, removed from Social Hall and installed in a shared study. No letter of explanation or telephone call was made to my parents and it was left to me to queue up one evening at the only telephone box in the whole school, tearfully, to tell them what had happened. I was so lonely that night, but CVP could not see that anything could be done and I had to brave it out.

Disgraced as I was, I never did recover in the eyes of that new Social tutor. For the rest of my years under his rule, apart from a consolation appointment as a Social prefect in my last term, he never gave me as much as a smile or a word of encouragement. Looking back, I suppose it was early in the days of modernisation, and just as well, but that didn't help me at the time.

Most of the time I managed to avoid him, and made good friends with several boys of my year, mainly from other Socials, who respected, even worshipped, their Social tutors and sympathised with me for the way I had been treated. As I have said, boys were forbidden to go visiting in the evenings as it was time for a curfew while we did our prep, but there were plenty of other occasions, especially during the long Sundays when we all got together during the daytime. There was no television then of course, but some Socials had radios and record players. We were allowed out too, on our bikes. It wasn't far to Abingdon, the nearest town, and we used to take the girls from St Helen's out to tea (it was more than our life was worth to be reported for being in a pub!). I became particularly fond of one girl called Jennifer and discovered a way to see more of her, legally too. One of the younger dons who hailed from Fife, started a Scottish reel club which happened two evenings a month in the gym. When some of us suggested that it would be more successful with female partners, he agreed, and arranged for a dozen girls to be bussed out from Abingdon. Needless to say, Jennifer was one of them! We actually became quite good, and I frequently volunteered when, very occasionally, someone suggested an eightsome reel or Petronella at some dance or other.

Then there was all the practice and care necessary to pass Cadet Corps inspections. I was a very keen army cadet and really looked after my uniform. I learned what 'spit and polish' really meant, and could see my face reflected in the toecaps of my boots. We would drill on the square, shoot on the range, learn how to read a map and even go on realistic exercises in nearby rough country. I loved all of that and in the end was promoted to Sergeant.

All this time I concentrated on my work and did well as the various exams came along. Fortunately, my Social tutor never taught me, so I had less and less to do with him. He had no interest in rowing, while for me all the happy hours that I spent on the river began to bear fruit. I used to cycle the couple of miles to the boathouse and came to long for those afternoons, sculling on my own under the weeping willows or rowing as a member of the Social crew. I shone in the junior sculls and our boat did well in the Bumping Races (Bumps, for short). This entailed all eight Social Fours lining up along the riverbank with a couple of boats' lengths between the stern of one boat and the bow of the one behind. At the sound of the cannon, all eight would set off, trying to 'bump' the rudder of the one in front (it was supposed to be a gentle nudge but wasn't always!). The competition took place after class on four successive summer evenings, and every time a crew bumped it would start the next day ahead of its victim. In this way, it was possible to start at fifth and finish up first ('Head of the River'). We usually did well, and not being sure when I was once asked whether we ever quite managed to achieve four bumps in four nights, I thought to revisit the college to find out. Records of the Bumps over many years are displayed in covered passage for all to see. But I have never been back.

I came to the notice of Llewellen Jones, the head rowing coach (nicknamed 'Lulu Jack'). He wore the hallowed pink scarf of the Leander Rowing Club and coached the 1st VIII. In my last year he invited me to be 'stroke' (the oarsman who sits nearest the cox and sets the all-important rhythm for the whole boat) in one of the Trial VIIIs. There were two of these, from which the 1st and 2nd VIIIs would eventually be chosen, one for the famous Henley Royal Regatta, the other for the 2nd VIIIs Marlow Regatta, both in July.

It went well through the Easter term, and when both crews were invited to come back a week early for the summer term for training, I found myself stroking the proposed 1st VIII. I queued for the phone box to tell CVP who was beside himself with joy. He proudly told all his legal pals after court and made sure that he would be free when the Henley dates came along.

Our crew entered upon many weeks of severe training, always beating the 2nd VIII and achieving some good times. We even had our own table in the dining hall, with special food to build us up! Then, about a month before the big event, there appeared a new figure. He wore the dark blue cap and scarf which showed he had rowed for Oxford University, and had been asked to give his valuable tips on how the 1st VIII could improve even more.

One afternoon, at the given signal ("Are you ready? – ROW!"), the 1st and 2nd VIIIs set off side by side down the river, closely followed by the college launch (called *Lusimus*, the first word of the school song, meaning 'we play'). I could see the two coaches talking to each other over the cox's head, as our boat crept into the lead,. After a bit, one called through his megaphone for both coxes to stop and to take their boats to the bank. This had never happened before and I wondered what was going on.

I soon found out. I was told to swap places with the stroke of the 2nd VIII, a very tricky manoeuvre in such fragile wooden boats, and a very embarrassing one at that, with two crews and all the occupants of the launch looking on. Having achieved this ungainly changeover, we set off again, and I finished the afternoon demoted. The head coach confided in me that, although I had good rhythm and rowed powerfully, my back appeared to break slightly as I came forward for a stroke, and the new man thought it wouldn't look good as our boat passed the expert spectators in the enclosures at Henley Royal Regatta.

Back at the phone box, there was no easy way to tell CVP, but he took it well. What neither of us knew at the time was that the same 'assistant coach' was to be taken on a week or two later as a mathematics don and simultaneously appointed to coach the 2nd VIII for the forthcoming Marlow Regatta. You guessed it. I finished up stroking the 3rd VIII, which got beaten in the first round of the lowly Pangbourne Regatta. My parents were there and I joined them for a picnic afterwards. Maybe I wasn't such a good oarsman after all.

There is a footnote to this episode, which caused me some satisfaction, when it became known that the man responsible for my misery had been a member of the crew that sank in the University Boat Race in March 1951!

As I approached the end of my time at Radley, I took up squash, tennis, even ballroom dancing, for although opportunities were rare, once a year there always appeared on the sports notice board an announcement that there would be a dance 'against' St Helen's on the following Saturday. This always happened in the huge and very grand hall where all important events took place, and we Scottish reelers were always there to dance with our girlfriends and even invite any lone 'wallflowers' for a waltz.

In the winter of 1952, remembering my performance as Brummy Crock, I joined the dramatic society in their performance of *Lady Precious Stream*, a Chinese play to be acted in its original format. Amongst others, this entailed having two actors called 'property men'. Having auditioned unsuccessfully for decent parts, I was appointed to be one of these. I had to stand dressed all in black, to make me as invisible as possible, on a chair at one side of the stage, facing the audience and holding out a rolled-up piece of black paper. This contained several pieces of torn-up white paper, which at a given cue I allowed to flutter to the floor. "Oh look, it's snowing," proclaimed one of the main actors. The audience laughed, I disappeared into the wings, and that was the end of my stage career.

In my final term, when I was a Social prefect and preparing to sit my exams for Oxford, there was great distraction caused by a series of fires throughout the college buildings.

Our own fire brigade, operated by half a dozen stalwart pupils who pushed a handcart loaded with water, pipes and sand managed at first. But then the whole art school, complete with painting materials, went up and the police were brought in. It turned out that the arsonist was actually a member of our fire brigade, a pyromaniac who enjoyed fighting the fires that he started himself!

Also during that time I came to know the school's careers master Mr Gilliat. In this capacity, he made it his business to meet and correspond with many of the captains of industry who might from time to time be on the lookout for promising young recruits. He made it plain to me that, if ever I was looking for a job, I should be sure to contact him.

By this time Nigel, who had followed me, was halfway up the school ladder in the same Social. He was doing well in cricket and hockey where he was in our Social team. I saw little of him as I swotted for my A levels in Latin and Greek and attended interviews for University and Hertford Colleges, both at Oxford. After leaving school at long last, I had to wait a while, but was in due course notified of acceptance by both colleges to read law. I chose 'Univ', simultaneously requesting that the college keep my place open for two years while I did my National Service. Others did it the other way round, but I thought it best to get it out of the way before going to Oxford and pursuing my chosen legal career. Little did I know how that decision was to change my whole life.

On 12 June 1953, during my last term, I had celebrated my eighteenth birthday. Nigel had four terms to go and David was to follow. Having finally got away, I have never been back to Radley, but I hear wonderful reports of that great school, which has obviously got better and better, as it has modernised, with an ever-growing reputation.

I have to say that neither my time at Radley nor all the money it cost CVP were wasted. There is no doubt that, whatever I thought at the time, the education – in the widest sense of the word – that I received there gave me a great start in life. I just feel that had it not been for two unfortunate staff changes during my four important years, I could have been one of those many who say how much they enjoyed their school days.

CHAPTER THREE

Around mid-September 1953, I received a buff envelope stamped OHMS telling me to hold myself in readiness to join the army. In due course, it said, I would be advised where and when to report with absolutely no further indication as to how long I would have to wait. With Christmas coming up I thought the best thing to do was to enjoy myself.

There was quite a large group of young men in West Sussex who were in the same position and a fair number of pretty girls who had also just left school. I didn't have much cash, but that didn't bother me. With the prospect of two years in the army looming, I made the most of that happy time.

About a dozen of us would meet up, usually in Brighton, at one of the coffee bars, or especially on Saturdays at the Pavilion, our favourite pub. It was a fun group and I am afraid we would get into quite a state. More than once I remember climbing into my little Ford Popular at nearly midnight and racing my friend Peter Dingemans back home to Steyning, about twelve miles away. He would always win because he had a fast Morgan, but sometimes it was quite close, and I have to admit that it was a pretty stupid, not to say dangerous, thing to do. If we had been seen by the authorities, we would have been in serious trouble, and rightly so.

Quite apart from these group get-togethers, I had a special girlfriend called Kay, who was not actually a member of our Brighton crowd. She lived at Stanmore, just outside London, and I saw her whenever I could, even if it meant missing out on our normal Saturday activities down in Sussex. In spite of seeing each other only infrequently, we grew quite close and her parents invited me to her eighteenth birthday party, which took the form of a dinner dance held at one of London's 'in' places of the time called 96 Piccadilly. We were quite a large table with plenty of good food and wine, making us all quite merry. During coffee, a message went round that Diana Dors was there and daring anyone to ask her for a dance.

Now, Diana Dors was the Blonde Bombshell of the day, some say England's answer to Marilyn Monroe, and very curvy with it. I could see her on the floor just finishing a dance with her boyfriend, and before I knew it, I was pushed towards her by some of the others. There was nothing for it but to blurt out my invitation for a dance. Lovely person that she was, she opened her arms in a quite inviting manner. Before long, I was whirling around, trying hard to make conversation, at the same time avoiding as far as possible looking too deeply down that famous cleavage. We didn't talk very much and I really don't know whether she enjoyed it. I rather doubt it though, because halfway through that number, she beckoned to her actress friend, Lana Morris, with whom I finished the dance before returning to my cheering table. I don't think I won anything for my dare, except a kiss from Kay, the birthday girl. My relationship with her didn't last though. Distance became a problem, and I lost out to other suitors, flocking around this beautiful blonde, who turned out to be a Dunhill heiress!

This fun time couldn't last for ever of course, and halfway through autumn, I received my instructions to report for basic training on 8 November at the barracks in Chichester, home of the Royal Sussex Regiment. That was all the letter said. Nothing about what to take, so I assumed that all would be provided, and in due course, so it proved. When my parents dropped me off, I was wearing a fairly trendy (at the time) blue blazer with brass buttons, cavalry twill trousers, suede shoes and a peaked cap. I didn't have them for long! Whisked away from me, they were locked in some far away store, to be reclaimed only if a day's leave was ever granted.

All replacement clothes were provided by the quartermaster. When I say all, it really was absolutely everything, including not only the thick battle dress itself but things with funny names like 'drawers, cellular, private soldiers for the use of' (underpants) and another thing called a 'housewife' (pronounced 'hussif'): a sewing kit. Of course, we had to sign for everything, and a short vicious little corporal gave us instructions as to how to clean and look after it. He showed us how to shine buckles, buttons and badges without getting Brasso all over the fabric of the uniform itself. Polishing our boots was a far more serious business than ever it had been at school. If, during an inspection, it was noticed that there was the slightest blemish or crack on a mirror-like toe cap, we would have to remove all the polish with sandpaper and white spirit, before starting all over again on both boots with plenty of spit and loads of polish!

Having explained all this to us, the corporal wound up with: "That's it then. Dismiss. Back to your quarters. When you get there, blanco everything else." By this, he meant us to use the khaki-coloured 'blanco' block supplied, using water and a brush, with which we had also been provided, on our belt, gaiters, ammunition pouches, and so on. One unfortunate recruit in my platoon took the instructions too literally and even blancoed his great coat! When it eventually dried, it was khaki all right, but also very stiff and extremely heavy as the poor soldier discovered when the nasty little corporal made him wear it on an early morning marching parade.

Eight weeks we were there, about thirty of us in my intake, made up of all sorts. I remember one particular lad, with a severely scarred face, who told us that it was all going to be a piece of cake. It turned out that this was in comparison with the previous three years of his life, which had been spent in prison! Another was the proud owner of a flick knife, which he proudly showed around. Not for long!

It wasn't actually that bad. We got used to 'Reveille', the 6am bugle that awoke us every morning, and to 'squaring' our bed. This entailed displaying every single item of our bedding and kit in a certain neatly folded way, for inspection, often by the Company Sergeant Major (CSM) himself. If it wasn't exactly right, the whole arrangement would be scattered by his boot, to be completely rebuilt for further inspection. I got pretty good at avoiding this sort of treatment, and the only one time I was punished was when I was sent to the guard room (a sort of twenty-four-hour prison) because I was overheard by the scary Regimental Sergeant Major talking about the Sussex Regiment instead of the *Royal* Sussex Regiment. This was unforgivable because we were all so proud of the Queen's patronage.

We came to learn drill and square bashing, how to clean a rifle and load an LMG (light machine gun, that wasn't at all light when you were humping it through trenches!). At meal times, all our food was ladled into our mess tin, a rectangular metal container, which we had to wash and polish immediately after use in case of a lightning inspection.

As we approached the end of our eight weeks' basic training, several of us were picked out as 'PLs' (potential leaders), and in due course were transferred to Canterbury. There we joined a special unit at HQ Home Counties where we were groomed to apply for Officer Cadet School (OCS) at Eaton Hall near Chester. We were only in Canterbury for six weeks, during which time the thirty PLs in my platoon competed for the Sword of Honour. Once again we were at the mercy of a small corporal, but this one was gay, and after a really tough time during which we were treated like the rawest of recruits, the Sword went to a PL called Collins whom the corporal much preferred to the rest of us!

We did well and most of us were duly sent for our final test to qualify for OCS. This test was called WOSB (pronounced 'wozbee'), which stood for War Office Selection Board. Applicants were drawn from all over the Home Counties Regiments and reported to a camp on Salisbury Plain just fourteen weeks after joining the army. The exam only took a day and was run by a group of officers with plums in their mouths, whose main aim seemed to be to conduct the tests and get back to their mess bar as soon as possible. There was a certain amount of theoretical work, during which we had to draw diagrams of an imaginary attack. This meant, for instance, putting lines on a large-scale Ordnance Survey map showing how we would deploy our men to dislodge a unit of the 'Fantasian' Army, which was supposed to be entrenched on a nearby hilltop.

After that we were taken in groups of eight or so to a muddy open trench twelve feet wide, which was supposed to represent a stream. I was told to get three of the men across the stream without any of them, or me, touching the bottom. The only equipment we were given was a thick plank, ten feet long, eleven feet of strong rope and something that looked like a javelin with a hook on the end. I worked out something that involved making a human bridge. It didn't work – all the men and equipment finished up in the bottom of the trench. But I got marks for ingenuity. Before leaving, I was given another of those little buff forms, so common in the army, which told me that I had passed. With it were enclosed a pair of bright blue 'flashes' to be worn on the shoulders of my uniform, signifying that I was a Potential Officer. There was also a brief instruction to take three days' leave and then to 'return to the Regimental Depot'.

After a lazy interlude at home, CVP dropped me back at the Chichester gates with my kit bag. Having left the latter in the guard room I walked, perhaps with a slight swagger because of my little blue shoulder flashes, to find the RSM and ask him where I would be staying. But I didn't find him – he found me. His voice hit me like a howitzer as he rounded the corner of a building behind me.

"YOU THERE! YOU WHAT'S NOT SWINGIN' YER ARMS. GET OVER 'ERE AT THE DOUBLE!" Well, there was no argument and I found myself running towards this man, who seemed no less fearsome than when I had first met him on the parade ground four months earlier.

Standing there at attention, it was a while before I could get a word in, but then I did manage to ask him where my quarters were and what he wanted me to do. The first part of the question was completely ignored, but he did tell me to: "Get yerself over to the Regiment Museum and polish everyfink made of brass until I tell yer to stop!"

This was not my idea of the duties required of a qualified Potential Officer, but once again there was no argument and, turning smartly about, I marched towards the museum. He hadn't finished with me yet though: "At the double!" he shouted. "And when yer get there take off them stupid blue dingle dangles!"

Once again, brought down to size…

Mercifully, this stay at Chichester Regimental HQ was short. I didn't enjoy being a spare part with no real duties and seemingly getting in everyone's way. They didn't know what to do with me, as the whole regiment had geared up for a spell of manoeuvres in Germany.

Once, during those awkward days, when CVP was in court at Chichester City Quarter Sessions (the family used to amuse ourselves by getting him to try and say that after three Jim Porters!), he brought Phyl along. At one o'clock, they collected me to go for a quick lunch and walk by the river; there was no time to get out my posh blazer, so I was wearing my uniform. I had their dog Candy on a lead as we set out along the towpath before stopping for a picnic. We had just settled down with our rug and sandwiches, when two young boys went by, and one said to the other: "Tim, look, there's a soldier." Tim gave a disdainful look over his shoulder at me, without even my regimental beret and badge, kneeling with the dog between my mum and dad. "Nah," he said. "That's not a proper soldier!" and kept walking. As my military career proceeded, and even afterwards, I was never allowed by the family to forget this little incident.

* * *

My first memory of Eaton Hall, except for the ugly building and the famous Golden Gates, was being 'fell in' and addressed by the CSM who told us: "From now on, I call you sir, and you call me sir, and you're the only ones who mean it!"

So it proved. Those instructors who were non-commissioned officers, with ranks from lance corporal up to RSM, had to call us, as budding Second Lieutenants, 'Sir'. But they had many ways of saying that little word, none of which contained even a tiny bit of respect, more a trace of sarcasm. We, of course, had to treat any real officers differently, not only calling them 'Sir' but also giving them a full salute whenever we passed them. This involved slipping our cane under our left arm, keeping that arm absolutely straight by our side, and saluting smartly with our right arm for a count of three paces. The officer, of course, was required to return the salute, but this was usually done in a very casual manner, because he had to acknowledge fifty or sixty salutes whenever he went anywhere.

That little cane we carried was the forerunner of the black and chrome 'swagger stick', complete with regimental silver knob, which we would qualify to carry on being granted our commission. In the meantime we had to manage with this piece of plain straight bamboo, about two feet long, which we had been required to purchase. It was carried at all times when not armed with our rifle, and became part of us. It was great for twiddling, throwing or conducting the band. Some people mastered the art of bouncing it end first on the tarmac in a way that it finished up neatly horizontal under their left armpit. I never did master this, partly because it splayed the end of the cane, and I didn't want to have to buy another one!

Against the background of more square bashing, training on the rifle ranges, theoretical work in the classroom, and nights in the trenches (our tea was always laced with bromide, apparently to curb any undesirable sexual urges which might arise), there were some very pleasant distractions. These came in the shape of establishments in nearby Chester, which we were permitted to visit in the evenings. One was called Bollands, another Quaintways. These days I suppose they would be called discos, but I am not sure the word had been invented then. Either way, they offered girls, booze and dancing to literally hundreds of cadets, all togged up in their best mufti (plain clothes) on a Saturday night. By this time I was receiving a useful weekly wage, which stretched to a couple of drinks and something to eat with one or other of the local girls who frequented these places. While some cadets spent most of the night in the city, I was usually back by eleven, being conscious of 'Reveille' early the next morning.

Our accommodation was a large Nissen hut, heated by a single wood-burning stove. Housing about three dozen cadets, it was, to say the least, sparse – but it sufficed. In the next bed was Teddy Goldsmith, whose brother, James, just at that time, hit the headlines. As we understood it from the papers, this wealthy young man wanted to marry a beautiful South American girl called Isabel Patino, but there were strong parental objections. What the papers did not say was that the couple were so determined that they left London secretly on their way to Gretna Green in Scotland where, unusually for those days, eloping couples could get married without the agreement of their parents. The first we knew of this was a loud knocking on the door of our hut at one o'clock in the morning. Teddy must have given them directions, but we never found out how the fleeing couple got past the guard! They spent the night together on the floor and carried on to Scotland the next morning for their wedding. It was all over the national press, but not one of them mentioned their secret stopover in our Nissen hut!

As I passed the various stages, and the hard-earned commission as a Second Lieutenant drew nearer, I wondered more and more where I was going to be sent as a newly qualified officer. I knew that, by this time, the Royal Sussex Regiment had been filled with the full complement of officers and men they needed for Germany and my enquiries revealed that I would be sent back to the barracks at Chichester until I was needed to go over there and help with their 'winter manoeuvres'. This sounded so boring that when an alternative arose, I leapt at the opportunity. This was, in a word, secondment. It meant that, once commissioned into my regiment, I would be lent to another, which was in greater need of me. The only snag was that on enquiring where that was likely to be, I was told that this would be drawn out of a hat. That hat was full of the names of the regiments, all over the world, which were offering positions to newly commissioned officers. The result – which was to decide the whole of my future life – was put up on a notice board. There, in the column next to Porter, it said: The Royal West African Frontier Force. Little the wiser, I consulted an atlas, to find that the British Territories in West Africa were Nigeria, the Gold Coast, Sierra Leone and the Gambia. The largest of these by far was Nigeria, and in due course I was told that I was to be posted to the 3rd Battalion of the Nigeria Regiment, currently based at a place called Abeokuta, sixty miles north of the capital, Lagos.

There was no time for further research as preparations for the famous 'passing out' parade were upon us. We were drilled from dawn till dusk until the whole company, about a hundred of us, moved, at a single word from the RSM, as one man. On the great day, in front of some General who had been allocated to Eaton Hall for the day, we proceeded as the band played the 'Eton Boating Song Slow March' through the huge Golden Gates, saluting the General as we went. The group of parents, including CVP and Phyl, filled with pride, applauded as their smart newly commissioned sons went by.

Second Lieutenant Porter

I was granted a week's leave, but there was no chance of enjoying myself this time. One day had to be spent filling in forms at Chichester, a day marked by my disappointment that the RSM had just departed for Germany. I had been looking forward to receiving and acknowledging his salute. Then the rest of the time was spent kitting myself out with cooler, tropical gear. Although I still had my heavy British Army uniform, by now with a precious 'pip' sewn to each shoulder to show my rank, everything had to be duplicated in the lighter-weight KD, Khaki Drill. This was made of 100% cotton and had to be washed and starched after each wearing. The uniform for the RWAFF consisted of a multi-pocketed jacket, baggy shorts, long socks, regulation boots and a bush hat. The hat was very smart with a wide brim turned up at one side, and a brass palm tree badge with a black/green feather. Then, of course, there was the famous Sam Browne belt and regimental swagger stick. Mine was ebony black with a silver tip and knob, embossed with the regimental palm tree emblem – I was so proud of it.

Seven and a half months after joining the army, this officer took a train to London and reported, complete with tin trunk and kit bag, to the top of a lift shaft leading down to a former tube station, at that time called the Goodge Street Deep Shelter. During the Blitz it had served as a refuge for hundreds of citizens. Now it was little more than a staging post, but at the same time, managed to be a forbidding place, with absolutely no daylight and a ventilation system that did little good. My reporting there was only a formality, and a few hours later, I was taking off in a military Hermes aircraft to begin the best part of my life thus far.

On the way, we refuelled at Malta and then flew through the night before landing at Kano in Northern Nigeria for more fuel and a change of clothing. I can still remember the wall of heat that hit me as I went down the steps from that plane, dying to get out of my prickly British uniform into my KD, shorts and all. The other thing that stuck in my mind was a proud and dignified African swathed in white cloak and turban, sitting high on a camel, with a four-foot long brass trumpet. We learnt that, for centuries gone by, the arrival of a camel train out of the desert was always announced by such a man, blowing long blasts that could be heard for miles, and the same tradition applied when a modern airliner was about to land.

We officers had a lightning tour of Kano and its ancient city, surrounded by a very high mud wall. High up in a minaret above the shining dome of the mosque, the faithful were being called to prayer. But after the long, slow overnight flight, it was difficult to form an accurate opinion of the place where, unknown to me at the time, I was to spend a happy eight years of my life.

How different and chaotic was our next port of call, with apparently the whole population of Lagos pushing, shoving and shouting at each other, from one side of the airport to the other. There was one other young subaltern bound for Abeokuta, and how glad we were to find a military driver, who loaded our gear into his khaki Land Rover. The road was single-track tarmac, so that when something came the other way, both vehicles put two wheels onto the dust and stones on their near side. The result was nil visibility for about a hundred yards and an alarming attack on our windscreen by a shower of stones of different sizes. Our driver, obviously used to it, would put one hand flat on the windscreen, saying that this would prevent it from shattering. It did seem to be effective too. There was another officer in the Land Rover, catching a lift back from Lagos. He was a Major, who turned out to be a company commander in charge of a hundred men. We called him 'Sir' and he was very friendly, full of information about the battalion and telling us to let him know if we would like to stop. We did tell him when we saw fruit for sale by the roadside, and the first black-and-white snapshot I sent home was of me holding on my shoulder a 30lb branch of ripe bananas that I had bought for 15 shillings (75p!).

There were five battalions of the Nigerian Regiment spread over the different provinces of that massive country (population then 33 million, now over 100 million). Every four years or so there would be a kind of general post, and each battalion would move on to another base. For the time being 3 NR (as our battalion was called) were happily installed in Abeokuta under the command of Col. D.H. Andrews, M.C., known to everyone as 'Crocus' (a nickname he acquired as a result of a stage appearance very early in his army career). It was to him that we reported after we had been shown to our quarters. He made it clear that our job was primarily to train the men in all aspects of battle and internal security. While the regiment had a famous reputation in World War 2 (notably in Burma), we had the distinct impression that with no imminent threat of war in 1954 the most likely role for our soldiers to play concerned local problems. Nigeria was a country made up of many tribes and religions, and occasionally trouble flared.

Our quarters were basic to say the least, with next to no hot water, a dribbling shower and only a thunderbox for a loo. This was a wooden structure whose name is self-descriptive; let's just say that, after each use, we threw in a shovelful of sand and sometime in the very early hours of each morning, a 'bayan gida' (behind the house) man would silently empty each one through a little door at the back. Usually he chose a time when we were safely asleep!

The good news was that each of us was given a 'boy', the local name for a batman, who did everything for us. He did not just wash, starch, iron, polish, and keep our quarters clean though. Each one was a soldier who trained with the rest, and was inevitably an excellent source of any rumours or scandals going on in the camp.

Of course, to speak to our boy, or indeed, to the whole company, it was a great help if we knew Hausa, the language of the soldiers, who hailed mainly from the Moslem north of the country. This was considered so important, especially on the battlefield, that officers were offered an addition to their pay if they attended lessons from the Mallam (teacher) and passed certain exams. I took advantage of this and my knowledge of the language not only brought in a little extra money but hugely improved my enjoyment of that great country and its people, both then and later.

Another way of improving my income was playing poker. My parents had often played after dinner with friends, using plastic chips for money, and I had picked up the rudiments of the game, including the all-important bluff. This stood me in good stead, and although the stakes were small I won enough to buy myself a whole new dinner suit when I got home. I didn't know then, but it was going to be very useful back in civvy street.

From time to time some of us were sent to Lagos for a week or two to assist with elections or to work on plans for internal security, such as the protection, in case of civil unrest, of key electricity substations, telephone exchanges, and so on. We used to look forward to these trips for a change of scene, and indeed, enjoyment. We could go to the clubs in the evening (in plain clothes of course) and at weekends make the most of the amazing beaches Lagos had to offer. On one occasion, when I was down there with fellow subaltern, Russell West, we decided to go surfing at Lighthouse Beach. It meant taking a seat on a motorised canoe to cross the main harbour, a bit scary because these boats were always very crowded and low in the water. You could actually see the grey shapes of large barracuda as they scavenged around the ships in the harbour and we didn't like to think what would happen if our overloaded boat hit a particularly high wave or wash from a passing liner! On arrival at a quiet little bay, we had to pay the boatman the equivalent of 10p and jump over the side holding our gear, including picnic and surfboard, above our heads. It was only a short walk to the main beach, where the surf looked really good, so we quickly changed and ran in with our boards. There was no one around for miles and we felt safe leaving our things in neat piles on the sand.

Figurehead on Lagos beach

In those days, our boards were still made of marine plywood, as they had been years ago in Devon. They were nowhere near as buoyant as those of today, but the surf was so high and strong that we could experience all the thrills and spills we needed. That day we surfed for a couple of hours, both burning our backs in the sun but not caring because we had such a great time. When we came out though, a surprise awaited us. Our clothes had been ransacked and both our watches and wallets had gone while we were buried in the waves. Looking around we came across a set of footprints leading back up the beach into the dunes at the top. Following them we were led straight to a grass hut where a young man lay sleeping. We surprised him and accused him in pidgin English (Hausa was of little use in the south) of stealing our things, but he denied it. There were some police on nearby Tarkwa Beach and I went to fetch one of them while Russell kept guard. There was no sign of our wallets or watches, and the man still claimed to the police officer that he had been asleep all afternoon.

We showed the police the prints on the sand and having given a full report, returned across the harbour to Lagos. We imagined that that would be the end of the matter, but fully three months later, we were summoned to give evidence in a Lagos court. We recognised the man in the dock and began to hope that the police might have actually recovered our valuables. We were dressed in full army officers' uniform and I suppose I reckoned we would make credible, not to say powerful, witnesses. Having given our names, rank and other details, I was told to wait outside the court, while Russell gave evidence. It wasn't long before he came out and I went in. After more questions about my occupation, the timing on the day in question and the state of the beach, the chief magistrate asked me how far from the sea we had piled our clothes. I said about forty yards, whereupon there was a hush and the magistrates conferred in whispers. Then the chief picked up his gavel, banged it on the desk and shouted, "Case dismissed!" As the defendant was freed and left the court, I was speechless and left to join Russell, who also couldn't understand what had happened. In the Land Rover on the way back to Abeokuta, we went through the questions we had been asked separately. It seemed that we had given similar answers about the time and the state of the beach, but when I asked Russell what he had said in answer to the one about the piles of clothes, he said he had told the court 'about 150 yards from the sea'. We never did agree who was right, but were quite obviously not seen as reliable witnesses. Neither did we discover whether our belongings had been recovered. Not hearing any further, we both had to make do with poor replacements, nowhere near as good as the ones we had brought from home.

Apart from training, the rifle range, fake battles and 'bush camp', the mess was the centre of our lives. Although only a flimsy structure, it contained a sitting room with comfortable armchairs, old newspapers and regimental silver on display (one of the prize items was a bugle which had been captured from the Japanese in Burma), a bar and kitchen. Locally made Star beer was the most popular refreshment, but stronger stuff was available as long as it was bought in by the Messing Officer. Each of us was appointed on a rotational basis to this position, which was quite scary, because, if a particular spirit or other item ran out, any one of the thirty odd officers could take it out on the MO of the week.

I did once find myself in serious trouble over curry. Hard to believe now, but I couldn't stand the stuff. Indeed, soon after my arrival in Africa, a harmless-looking piece of curried egg at a cocktail party had brought out a bright pink rash down the inside of both my arms and I had managed to avoid it ever since. Unfortunately, though, there was one occasion when a message came from the colonel that curry should be served in the mess at a Sunday lunch when he and Mrs Andrews would be joining us. Well, I used my position as MO that day to avoid having to eat it. I took Sergeant Sampson (the Mess Sergeant) onto one side and told him that, although the cook was providing green curried chicken with side dishes for everyone else, he was to serve me a ham salad. Placing myself at the end of the table far from the colonel, I would have got away with it, had he not decided to take a little walk around chatting to some of his National Services Officers of whom he was so fond. When he got to me and my cold ham, he could hardly speak – his face went red, just like a caricature of a British army colonel and he nearly exploded. How dare I abuse my position? I was to report to his office the next morning to explain myself.

That Monday morning, I really tried everything I knew, but had no chance. I received my punishment of seven days Extra Orderly Officer. This meant that, in addition to my normal duties, for a whole week I had to inspect the Guard at four-hourly intervals throughout the day and night, and also to check the security of the boundary fence. This meant a two-mile bicycle ride with a torch at midnight and again at four in the morning, before signing the book in the Guard Room and returning to bed in the hope of getting some sleep. I did learn to eat curry, and now it's my favourite!

Extra Orderly Officer

Like my fellow Subalterns, I really respected Colonel Crocus. He had the most distinguished record, and, had we been at war, we would have done anything he asked. Most evenings he would pop in for his whisky soda and stay for a chat. He particularly enjoyed the monthly Messing Nights, which at first were quite formal affairs, as we all dressed up in our 'monkey jackets' (mess dress) and behaved ourselves. That was until the port had been passed clockwise round the table, always returning to the Colonel at the head of the table, where the stopper was replaced in the neck of the decanter (till it went round again!).

After that though, all hell broke loose. Poker cards were put away and every kind of rumbustious game was played. One favourite was hicockalorum, which entailed one man, called the anchor, crouching against the wall with two or three others crouching similarly next to him, so that a line stuck out into the room. The rest of us then took turns to run and jump over the line, landing on the back of the anchorman against the wall, before crouching to make the line longer. One night the Colonel volunteered to take part as anchorman and by the time it was my turn there were nearly a dozen backs for me to clear before reaching him and the wall. Running at great speed, I somehow tripped and crashed into the very first man, thus pushing the whole line a foot or so, and the Colonel went through the wall. It was only made of plasterboard and fortunately the outer cladding was more sturdy and prevented the CO from finishing up in the garden!

On another special occasion, when I was again Messing Officer, I had this idea of rigging a series of lights in the tall palm trees, which stood in a perfect circle on the lawn in front of the Mess. The Colonel came to inspect, liked the idea, but suggested that I used coloured bulbs. When I told him we didn't have any, he told me sharply to draw paint from the Quartermaster's Stores in four different colours to use on the bulbs. I instructed Sergeant Sampson accordingly and thought no more of it till the Colonel arrived with Joan, his lovely wife. He stopped at the entrance, looked around and then glared at me with a look of amazement on his face. Not realising at first what was the problem, I followed the direction in which his hand was pointing, up at the lights in the trees. Oh my God! Every fourth bulb seemed to be missing. Each one had been painted jet black!

One of the more senior officers was Giles Devereux, a Major, who was in charge of HQ Company (Admin). He was huge fun and always joined in, but had one serious problem. He had come up through the ranks over many years, and only just managed to conceal his disdain for us young public schoolboys who had got our commissions after only a few months. After heavy nights in the Mess, and when the booze got to work, he used to express this view in jocular fashion and we came to expect it. One particular night though, I laughed a bit too loudly and Giles, pretty far gone as he was, took exception to it. Pushing back his chair, he came for me and I only just escaped his lunge. Next thing, he seized a golf club from a bag in the hall, and holding it high above his head, announced that he was going to 'kill Porter'! I fled through the garden and shut myself into the first room I reached, locking the door behind me. The window was open, but protected from thieves by a strong grill made of expanded metal. This didn't deter Giles though. Turning the golf club round, he stabbed it handle first through one of the holes, hoping to get me. Well, I was far out of range on the other side of the room, but this was the room of the Medical Officer who had an African grey parrot, whose perch was close to the window. Knocked off by the golf club, he was found dead on the floor the next morning by his owner – but Giles knew nothing about it. Neither did Porter, of course!

Off duty, and towards the end of my secondment, I became great friends with the Colonel's family, mainly because of their pretty seven-year-old daughter Diana. Eventually it became quite a joke, but on one occasion, over lunch in front of the Colonel and his wife, she and I exchanged notes, with her parents' knowledge I must say, that we would get married when she was 21. Needless to say, that never happened, but I am still in touch with her, her husband and lovely family in Winchester.

I also took up fishing. When we went to Bush Camp, it was at a place called Eruwa on the banks of a tributary of the Niger River. Therein lurked 'Giwan Ruwa' (Hausa for 'Elephant of the Water'), which were in fact Niger perch. They were indeed huge. The Colonel's record was 52 lb; mine was less at 46 lb, but quite a fighter and wonderful to eat. We also shot wild guinea fowl for consumption in the Mess, and a nearby European farmer used to invite us to shoot the bush fowl (a kind of partridge) that ate his pineapples. The trouble was that he paid us in pineapples too, and we soon got fed up with the things!

After about six months, Major Whitehead, CO of 'C' Company came to the end of his tour and went home. To my surprise, I was promoted to Company Commander, and simultaneously became an Acting Captain – no extra pips on my shoulders but a bit more money. This meant that I could pay £55 per month into my London account. I hardly ever used that chequebook, so the balance built up to a respectable figure for those days. Dick Jones joined me from another company as my second in command to help me train and control a hundred men. Dick and I got on famously. The only thing I didn't know, but discovered over fifty years later, was that he kept a diary about most things that went on, some of them quite embarrassing! He had it printed, complete with old photographs, and I now have a copy that I bought from him for two litres of whisky. It is hilarious and entitled *The Backbone of the Battalion*.

In spite of all the fun we had, I now found that serious responsibilities lay upon me. True, I had an excellent Company Sergeant Major in Ibrahim Kano, who shouldered most of the soldiers' personal problems (many of them had wives and families living in the 'lines' in the residential part of the camp). However, most mornings he marched several men before me, charged with a variety of crimes, mainly to do with money, women or the locally made palm wine. Penalties ranged from stoppage of leave, pay or, occasionally, demotion, and the CSM always stood behind the accused, making signs at me to indicate what the man deserved!

There was a huge amount for these men, mainly illiterate, to learn, but they were well aware of the chance that the army gave them, and threw themselves into it. Very good soldiers they made too, and to see them all lined up in their red waistcoats and fezzes was quite a sight. They would march for miles in temperatures of 40°C, singing rhythmic songs to keep themselves (and me!) going. Although their .303 rifles were totally unfamiliar, indeed quite frightening to some, they would listen and learn till they became good marksmen. I used to take them out for whole days to the range, where I would split them, one half to fire, the other to man the sand butts, where the spent bullets would finish up after passing the targets. These were two or three hundred yards away, and signals were made back to me with long sticks like lollipops indicating how each rifleman had scored.

This all usually went smoothly except one time when I had eight men lying down ready, each with five rounds loaded in his rifle and the report came through on the field telephone that those manning the butts were prepared. At the top of my voice I shouted to the eight, "ARE YOU READY? RAPID... FIRE!" Even as the din broke out with forty bullets screaming away I saw, in the distance, a figure climbing up the sand banked up behind the targets. "STOP FIRING. STOP FIRING!" I yelled, but it was hopeless. Nobody could hear me above the noise. The figure disappeared, alive or dead, I had no idea. When peace at last descended, I furiously wound the handle of the range phone to ask the Sergeant in charge of the butts what the b_____ h___ was going on, and he calmly said that someone had thrown

Private Amadu's beret up in the sand and he had gone up to get it. Apparently he had survived, but I doubt whether I would have survived a Court Marshal!

In April 1955, it was time to move stations to Enugu in the Eastern Region (years later to be briefly called Biafra during the awful war of that name). As can be imagined, it was the mother and father of all packing exercises, but we managed to load all the hundreds of crates onto the trucks, which set off before us. We were to take the men by train, a journey of nearly a thousand miles, because the only railway went via Kaduna up in the Northern Region. It took us three days, and was uneventful except it was during that journey that the train jerked to a sudden stop and I saw my first dead body. The railway company employed men to walk along the track, many miles of it, checking sleepers and tightening bolts. Sometimes, because they got tired, they needed a little sleep, and, so that they could hear the inspector coming along in his little hand operated truck, they rested their heads on the rails. It didn't work for one poor man. He was so fast asleep, he didn't even hear our huge train coming and our driver couldn't stop in time. There was quite a delay that day.

I shared my accommodation at Enugu with Bev Mott who had joined the battalion by then. It was much more comfortable and we even had a bath, as long as our boy made a fire to heat the water. It was quite a way from there to the office and we usually walked together while Bev enjoyed smoking one of his favourite Senior Service cigarettes. That went on for a month or two, but one day he said to me on the way that he wanted to give up. He stubbed out the cigarette he was smoking and gave me the remainder of the packet, about fifteen I would say, making me promise never to give them back. I had never smoked in my life, but I had five of those cigarettes before lunch and another two before the end of the day. I still don't understand why, but that started me off, and I smoked on and off, though never heavily, till the late sixties, when I too gave up, preferring a pipe. As long as I knew him, Bev never touched another one! Eventually, I gave up my pipe too, as my reader will discover.

One day soon afterwards Bev and I were at the bar in the Enugu Club, when we fell into a conversation with a fellow from Outward Bound, a marvellous charitable organisation that provided outdoor holidays for young people. He was visiting to buy stores for the hostel where he was based at Buea in the foothills of Mount Cameroon. Would we like, he said, to go back with him and climb the mountain? (Just under 14,000 feet!) We had no leave due, but Colonel Crocus was great as usual, and within twenty-four hours we were bumping through the bush in our new friend's Jeep. I left Dick in charge of 'C' Company.

On our way to the border, we saw more wild game than during all the rest of my time in West Africa put together. There were plenty of deer and antelope plus different kinds of monkey, two hyenas, several giraffe and a huge python that easily stretched from one side of the track to the other. When I saw my first elephant in the wild, I really wished that I hadn't forgotten my little camera in the rush.

74

We had only been given three days' leave, so, very soon after our arrival, we were introduced to the guide who was to take us up the mountain the next morning.

We were certainly fit from long marches and playing lots of squash, but that climb – first through steaming jungle and then, more steeply, in the blazing sun – took it out of us. Eventually though, we reached hut three, just below the summit, cooked ourselves something on a camp fire and went to bed, looking forward to the final assault. The next morning, it was blowing a gale and to our dismay, our guide said it wasn't safe to go the last hundred feet. We told him we hadn't come all this way to *nearly* climb Mount Cameroon. He said it was up to us, and we set out on our own, lying on our stomachs and doing the 'leopard crawl' we had learnt so well in basic training. Quite soon, and safely, we reached the top and looked down into the crater, which looked harmless enough. We didn't stay long, and as we turned away, I picked up a small piece of lava and put it in my backpack.

"What's that for?" asked Bev.

"To put on the mantelpiece when I get home." I said.

He thought that was really wet, and said so, but I didn't listen. Later, as our toes really began to hurt going down the steepest slopes, he asked me if he could have a piece of my lava, but I told him to go back and get his own! Mine did indeed sit on the mantelpiece of my parents' house in Sussex for many years, but then they moved and it got lost. I am still disappointed, especially because I later heard that the mountain had been re-measured and was now officially just over 14,000 feet. Although I am certainly no expert in such matters, my informant at the time told me that this meant I could apply for membership of the Alpine Club. I never did!

That trip was unforgettable and I will never regret having undertaken it, in spite of the fact that, during my unexpected absence, Dick took it upon himself to entertain my girlfriend of the time. She was called Ivy, and was very special, not least because there were very few single girls around in Enugu. Dick said he thought he was being helpful (he took her home at 2am!) but I thought it was a bit of a cheek. After all, I was his Company Commander, and he should have asked permission!

To be given such responsibility at such a young age certainly did me good, but more than that, I revelled in being my own master. True, there were senior officers above me, but as far as my Company was concerned, most of the time I really could do my own thing. I took frequent decisions, some of them quite serious, in that they concerned the success and wellbeing of so many soldiers, often with families. Above all, I learnt that, should one of those decisions turn out to be a mistake, it was undoubtedly best to admit it and to start again. Such a useful lesson for the years ahead!

* * *

As May 1955 came to an end, and my return to England drew near, I began to have second thoughts about university. I had now been self-sufficient for nearly two years and had even saved several hundred pounds, never having asked

CVP for any money, except perhaps in the very early days when I had to 'kit up'. I really hated the idea of going 'back to school' and asking him to see me through Oxford. I knew it would be a disappointment to him if, after all, I didn't study to be a barrister, but eventually I plucked up courage and wrote to him, telling him how I felt.

In those days, letters from deep in the West African Bush to West Sussex, travelling by mail boat, took three weeks, however many stamps you applied. It was, of course, the same the other way round, hence my letter crossed with one from CVP. 'My Dear Boy,' it started, and went on to say that, as things were at the office, he sincerely doubted whether he was going to be able to see me through university. 'I know this will come as a disappointment to you…,' he wrote. We received our respective letters, a few days apart. It was only later that I discovered what had happened. The elderly senior partner of his firm of solicitors had made a serious error, resulting in it being sued. The amount was so large that the firm's insurance wouldn't cover it, and each partner, including CVP, who spent his time in court and had no part in the error, had to pay their share. Quite late in his career this was a serious blow to him, resulting in his letter to me. I have always thought mine to him must have brought considerable unexpected relief.

I did briefly consider staying on in the army, which I loved so much, but I realised that re-joining the Royal Sussex Regiment would be entirely different from life in Africa, so I decided against it and set about making other plans.
Within a week I had written to University College at Oxford

resigning the place I had worked so hard to gain, and then to my old careers master, asking if he could help me find a position in the world of commerce.

My last couple of months at Enugu were spoiled by illness; I had contracted amoebic dysentery which dragged me down. Much as I looked forward to going home, and with my friends envying me so, I found it hard to celebrate. There were farewell dinners and Company tributes, but I was losing weight fast and only wanted to get on that plane. When 23 August 1955 finally arrived though, emotions prevailed. Hugging the Colonel's little girls, receiving the final salute from CSM Ibrahim Kano and saying goodbye to my closest friends, it finally got to me. Dick came to the airport to see me off, and I am afraid it was a tearful twenty-year-old Acting Captain that finally mounted the steps of that military transport plane.

CHAPTER FOUR

I n spite of my poor health, I quickly slotted into life back at home. Most of my friends were either finishing their time in the services, or coming down from their universities for the summer. My parents, with whom I had kept in fairly regular touch, seemed unchanged, and Phyl's healthy Yorkshire cooking soon got me strong again. I didn't want to spend too much time, though, without doing something about my future.

Just then I received a reply from the careers master. He advised me that ICI (Imperial Chemical Industries Ltd), then one of the ten biggest companies in Britain, were offering trainee positions to school leavers who had completed their National Service, but had chosen not to take a degree. He also gave me an introduction to the personnel director of ICI Paints Division, famous for their Dulux brand, based in Slough, Buckinghamshire. The interview with him went well, and I was offered a position at £390 per annum to commence on 1 October 1955. CVP was thrilled that I had landed a job with such a famous and well-respected company, an opinion well supported by a further letter received from them three weeks before I was to join. It said that there had been a general increase of salaries throughout the company of 5%, which meant that my annual salary had gone up to £409 and 10 shillings per annum even before I started! Nowadays, that seems a puny amount, but at the time I was well satisfied.

I had returned from Nigeria with nearly £250 in my account, but had blown some of it on that new dinner suit, several months of living it up that summer, and a little Morris 8 convertible built in 1934 (one year before me!). The car was Post Office red, with a rather torn hood and a driver's door that was apt to fly open if not held in place by my right elbow!

In the absence of an electric starter motor, the only way to get it going was to insert the starting handle into a hole over the front number plate, and 'swing' it in a clockwise direction till it sprang to life. This wasn't always successful, but early one windy morning in late September 1955, she did start like a bird. That was the day I first set out for my new digs, the back bedroom in the house at 123 Langley Road, Slough, belonging to Mr and Mrs Buxton who had agreed to let it to me for £1.15 shillings (£1.75) a week (Monday to Thursday), including a hearty cooked breakfast. It was only a ten-minute drive to the ICI Paints factory, and Mrs B, who took a great interest in my affairs, always saw to it that I left her front door with enough time to spare, in case I had to ask her husband to help me push start the Morris!

In a certain wind direction the whole of Slough smelled of paint and varnish. Still does, I believe. There were hundreds and hundreds of people who turned up on my first Monday morning at that huge factory, and it took me a while to park and walk to the personnel department where a desk awaited me. After a very genuine welcome from the director who had appointed me, I was given a job that was to bore me for the next three months. It entailed the careful examination and collation of results achieved by a large number of company employees who had attended various specialist courses. Whether they had attended these within the paints division itself, on day release or at night school, it was important to the personnel department to know how they were doing, and it was my duty to present a daily report. There were of course no computers in those days to help create spreadsheets and the like. I never could type, so the whole thing had to be written out by hand.

It was a great atmosphere, though, and I made some good friends inside and outside my department. Every day, we used to meet up for a good lunch in the canteen for which we had to pay one shilling and sixpence (7.5p). There I first fell for Lois; it was through a cloud of steam, because she was a trainee canteen manageress, and at the time was standing behind the counter replenishing a huge urn of coffee. I suppose she couldn't see me very well either, but when I asked her out for supper and pictures in the Slough Odeon, she did say yes.

That first date with her was not a complete success. The cinema had its own restaurant, where we sat and ordered before the film. I forget what I chose, but whatever it was, I decided that it needed tomato ketchup. Even as I chatted her up, I gave the plastic bottle some good shakes, not knowing that each one deposited a red globule on my specially washed and ironed white shirt. Lois stopped me as soon as she noticed, but the damage was done!

That was the first of many laughs we had together, and a romance was born. Whenever possible, we met up, but not at 123 Langley Road. Mrs B would never have approved! Lois lived with her dad in a village by the river Thames near Maidenhead, and I often ran her home, stopping on the way at the Bel and Dragon (sic) pub near where she lived at Bourne End. There was one very foggy evening when I could hardly see the road ahead, so we spent longer in the bar than usual, hoping for it to clear. Slowly, everyone else left till we were alone; it was chilly, so we sat together on a sheepskin rug in front of the dying fire. We were only hugging each other, well, and kissing a bit too, when the landlord walked in to turn out the lights because he thought everyone had gone. He wanted to know what the blankety blank we were doing. Didn't we know it was after closing time and would we blankety blank get out of his pub! Not waiting to tell him he should have rung the bell, we scrambled to our feet and went out into the fog, which was now even thicker. Laughing as we were, the incident didn't worry us a bit and we went back there often, as our relationship became closer and closer. Sometimes I would even take a late lunch in the canteen, so that I could sit with Lois when it was time for hers. After all, she was much prettier than the lads with whom I normally shared a table!

It was my fault that it all came to an end. I asked her to go to a dance with me. We both enjoyed ballroom dancing, but had never done it together; I wore my new dinner jacket, and she one of those New Look dresses so popular in the fifties. She looked fabulous, but something bothered me. It seems stupid now, but her face, though not quite so flushed, was just the same as I had originally seen it through the steam. Halfway through a quickstep, and half joking, I asked her why she didn't wear make-up like the other girls. That did it. Breaking away from me in the middle of the dance floor, she was furious and told me through angry tears that, if I didn't like her as she was, I'd better find someone else, and would I please take her home. This blew into a full-scale argument, and no amount of apology seemed to assuage her. After that she managed to avoid me, even in the canteen at lunchtime, and never spoke to me again. I tried everything I knew, but in vain. I was distraught. Of all the occasions I later kicked myself for saying the wrong thing at the wrong time, that unfortunate remark would always be in the top ten. (Having said that, maybe in the medium to long term the result wasn't at all bad!)

Soon afterwards I was sent from the personnel department to go on a course round the whole factory, including the technical service department, to learn about how to make and use top-quality paint. It started with a night shift, when I was told to report at 11pm to the section leader in the ball mill shed. There were about twenty of these mills, each one consisting of a massive cast-iron horizontal cylinder, one third full of 6-inch steel balls. Having climbed up to a platform in order to add over a ton of varnish, chemicals and pigments through a hatch with a heavy trapdoor, the operator would close it, using a huge spanner to tighten the nuts. He would then climb down and press a button, which started a powerful electric motor. This would rotate the mill, sometimes for as long as twenty-four hours, until the contents were ground to a smooth paste, suitable for the next stage of the manufacture of the paint itself.

All this was explained to me by the foreman in charge when I came on duty, dressed up in regulation overalls. I helped him lift the heavy sacks, and between us we emptied about thirty of them into the hatch of one of the mills. These were followed by ten 5-gallon drums of varnish and some dark grey pigment. We had finished tipping them in by 2am when he called a halt for a tea break in the canteen, but before we left, he rested the door on the hatch, only loosely securing it, because there was still one ingredient to add on our return.

While we were away, a helpful colleague who had already had his tea, noticed the trapdoor was in place as he passed and, in order to save time, went down and hit the start button, before continuing on to his own area. Round and round that mill spun with nobody noticing amongst all the others in that vast and noisy factory that the contents were escaping. Fortunately, the trapdoor had been secured just enough to prevent the steel balls themselves coming out, but by the time we came back the floor, the ceiling and several adjoining mills were covered in the other contents. By the time we could reach the stop button, we too were covered. Battleship grey, I remember, was the colour description. A serious inquiry followed, but fortunately I escaped without blame.

My technical course soon followed and took six months. By the end of it, I could spray cars and boats, brush paint buses and houses, de-rust, degrease and paint by a dipping process any amount of special machine parts in any amount of specially formulated products. Each process and paint was fully described in a 'Technical Bulletin' and I had to take these home, to learn word for word, ready for tests, which were sprung on me from time to time.

About six months into my training, I teamed up with two other lads and moved into Vicarage Cottage, Stoke Poges. It was sad leaving Mrs B, but she did understand and I popped back now and again to see her. She had found a new tenant without difficulty.

Great fun as the cottage turned out to be (the vicar in the main house was tolerant of most of the goings-on), it was considerably more expensive. My salary had crept up to nearly £430 a year by then, but I was still always short of cash and remember one lunchtime when two of us walked into Slough for half a pint and a sandwich in the Plough Inn. When we came out, it was pouring with rain. I didn't own a mac, so I dived into a nearby Millets to buy one. Unfortunately, it was £7 and 10 shillings (£7.50). No credit cards then, and I couldn't be sure that I could safely sign a cheque for that amount, so I bought that mac on hire purchase, with a down payment of 30 shillings (£1.50) and the remainder to be paid at 8 shillings and 6 pence (42.5p) a month! That's how short I was at that time.

I was getting even more bored with my weeks of training and thankfully, about a year after I joined, I was given permission to apply for a vacancy I had spotted in the export sales department. There followed a series of interviews, culminating in the most important one with the export sales director, an extremely important man. It was going fine, when, out of the blue, he suddenly asked me when I did my thinking. Without hesitation, I said, "Usually when I'm driving, sir." I thought he was going to explode, as he almost shouted at me that, when I was at the wheel, I should be doing absolutely nothing other than trying to drive safely, and certainly better than the next man.

I survived though, and was invited to sit down with the export sales manager to countersign my form of appointment to his department. I looked through it carefully, and paid special attention to the section about overseas postings. It asked whether I had ever been overseas, and I wrote: Yes, Nigeria. Would I be prepared to represent the company overseas? Yes, I wrote. Is there any country where I would not be prepared to go? Yes, I wrote, Nigeria. I reckoned I had seen enough of that country and liked the idea of getting to know somewhere else, perhaps a little more exotic. I signed the form.

Although I never did travel there, I was put in charge of the section whose job it was to export paint of all kinds and colours to the Caribbean and Central American markets. The actual selling was done by our manager who flew there several times a year, quoting for big paint contracts and appointing local agents. These agents were vital tools in the territories themselves and other major paint manufacturers were constantly trying to persuade the best ones to change allegiance.

This was when I was involved in another of the unfortunate situations to which I seemed to be prone. It all started with a very large order we received from our agent in San Jose, Costa Rica, for several different colours of Dulux gloss and emulsion to paint a large new hotel. It was the result of a trip by our manager and my job was to draw up a confirmation to be sent to our agent, advising the various prices and expected date of shipping. It was only a slip but I carelessly signed one without noticing that, instead of 2,000 gallons of white, we would be sending him 2,000 gallons of shite.

You wouldn't expect a grown business man out in Central America to make a big fuss about an obvious typing error, but this one did. He wrote to the manager, who called me into his office for a dressing down. He said I should not be so careless and that I was to write immediately, apologising to his valued Costa Rican agent for my mistake.

It got worse! We had Dictaphones in the office, each fitted with a microphone so that we could dictate letters onto a floppy disc. This disc was sent to the typing pool in a file, which was in due course returned to the writer for his signature prior to dispatch. Well, I dictated a letter of abject apology onto one of these discs, and just for fun, I added a postscript: 'And if you like, I'll come out there and kiss your backside.' Whether I was ill when the letter came back for signature, or maybe I had a day off, I don't remember. All I do know is that my assistant, who sat at the next desk, signed all my mail on my behalf and dispatched it in my absence, without noticing that the young lady in the typing pool had typed the PS in full!

I like to think that this regrettable incident had nothing to do with my posting away from Slough, but not many months later, I was told that I was to be posted to a new ICI company which had been established overseas, responsible for selling all the products of the thirteen manufacturing divisions of ICI. Where was that? Lagos. Where was that? Yes, Nigeria!

Since losing my lovely Lois, I had been without a girlfriend in Slough, but had found a brilliant one at home in Sussex. To some extent the old gang had reassembled, meeting together, especially on Saturdays, in coffee bars and pubs in the morning and perhaps one of the hotels that held dances in the evening. We dressed up for these, sometimes in evening dress, and the girls looked wonderful in their fashionable dresses and high heels. The ballroom dancing would look very dull to today's youngsters, but we loved taking turns to dance the foxtrot, old-fashioned waltz

My smart Triumph Gloria

or perhaps the samba, with different partners. Towards the end of the evening, the band would always play the conga and the Charleston, which we loved. Then, after the lights had dimmed, each guy would find his own girl for a smoochie last waltz, before climbing into their old cars, slightly the worse for cheap wine or cider, to go home. I had a bigger and more comfortable Triumph Gloria by then and often made a small deviation for a quick kiss and cuddle somewhere in the hollows of the South Downs, before dropping my partner home at about one in the morning.

While I at first had no steady girl of my own, Peter Dingemans (who was to become an Admiral) always came with a Polish girl, who lived in Brighton, called Barbara Hulanicki. She was about nineteen, and doing well at art school. Sometimes, when I danced with her, I began to hear about her young sister who was nearly seventeen, still at school, called Beatrice.

Dancing with Barbara, my future sister in law.

Although B (for Beatrice) was not allowed to come out at night, she did go to the coffee bars and one day, through Peter, I set eyes on her for the very first time. I had better not say it was love at first sight. She wouldn't approve of such soppiness, but she was easily the most lovely girl I had ever seen, and I did everything I could to make her mine. I used to pick her up whenever I could at the school gates and several times even wrote her essays for her (she always got good marks!). She lived with her mother, Barbara and their younger sister Biba in a beautiful flat in Grand Avenue, Hove, next to Brighton. There, I slowly became accepted into a very female household, and was eventually allowed to take B out on Saturday evenings. I was so proud of her, and at the first opportunity took her to meet my parents. They had met several of my girlfriends over the years, but could tell that this one was special (even though she was a foreigner!), and she was welcomed into their home more and more often.

Although our relationship was not always smooth at first, we became a regular couple, and it was still like that when B was sent to a finishing school for young ladies called The Cygnet House in Queen's Gate, London. She hated it there, being taught all the prim things expected of a debutante (although she was to avoid attending Queen Charlotte's Ball to become one). It was a very forced existence, and she teamed up with similarly minded girls from other parts of the world, to rebel whenever she could.

With B at one of her London Balls.

Sometimes I would dress up and partner her at one of her balls, but was of course worried sick that, stuck out in Slough, I might lose her to one or other of the smooth young London men who cruised around the West End, hoping to pick up a Cygnet at some official reception or other. I was saved by a list drawn up by the principal and parents, which made clear with which men each girl would be allowed to leave the The Cygnet House. Apart from one other brief entrant, I was the only one on B's list during the whole year she spent at Cygnets, so I always had her to myself!

It wasn't all plain sailing, though. In 1957 there came strict petrol rationing, and it was all I could do to procure enough to get my car from Sussex to Slough and then back after my week's driving to work. My much bigger six-cylinder car (complete with a chrome gallows mascot and hanging body on top of the radiator) drank petrol greedily. To drive into London seventeen miles each way was therefore out of the question, and the trains didn't run late enough back to Slough. There was only one thing for it. Rather than not see B till the weekend, I bought myself a second-hand bicycle. It took me an hour and a quarter each way to see her, and it was a pretty exhausting ride too. If that wasn't love, I didn't know what was. As if to prove it, if the wind was behind me on the way back along the A4 at night, I would heartily sing the latest hit called 'True Love', a favourite song by Bing Crosby and Grace Kelly in *High Society* at the time. (Sorry B, that is soppy, but I'm not making it up!)

While we never became officially engaged, we were so happy together and were invited everywhere as a couple. I think it is true to say that we both expected to marry one day, but with my career still in its infancy and B getting a good modelling job with Mr Teasy-Weasy, the famous hairdresser in London's West End, there seemed to be no hurry. That was when, out of the blue, just before Christmas 1958, I was told that I was being sent far away to West Africa for a tour of fifteen months.

Apart from anything else, it was a strict rule within ICI that new recruits for overseas companies could not marry during their first tour. Furthermore, not only would it have been a big rush to arrange a wedding within two months, but we had already decided, with amazing good sense, that we would not rush into anything.

So it came about that, early in February 1959, B came to Euston Station to see me off on the boat train to Liverpool.

There was another person on the station that day, called Peter Kent, who was to play a big part in the next bit of my life. All on his own, with a smart briefcase and a roving eye, awaiting the departure of the train, he espied me and this beautiful girl saying a lingering goodbye. Later he told me that, lost in the crowd, he did not actually see which one of us got on the boat train, so he spent the first fifteen minutes of the journey struggling up and down the rocking train, only to be disappointed to find it was not that pretty girl, but me in my blue blazer!

When we boarded the Elder Dempster Line Mail Boat *MV APAPA* bound for Freetown in Sierra Leone, Takoradi, Ghana, and Lagos, Nigeria, Peter was quick off the mark joining the crowd with the most sexy girls. Following my recent sad parting, I didn't do that, but after a few lonely evenings, I did sit at dinner with a sweet freckly girl from Paisley called Evelyn, who was going out to Lagos with her new baby to join her husband. This seemed pretty harmless, especially when compared with all Peter's goings-on all day (and night!), and I didn't see much of Evelyn except at meal times. However, it did go terribly wrong when we reached Freetown. Evelyn had an uncle who worked there, who had arranged to come aboard to see her and the new addition to the family. After breakfast that day, she asked me if I could sit with the baby in her cabin while she went up to meet her uncle, and I readily agreed.

Two things happened then. First the baby started yelling, so I had to pick it up and rock it in my arms. Then, unknown to me, she and her uncle missed each other when he came aboard. The first I knew of this was a knock on the cabin door. When I opened it, there was this big, bearded, Scottish uncle who was, to say the least, confused to find this complete stranger in his niece's cabin, cuddling her new baby! Having invited him to sit on the bed, I did my best to explain, but there followed ten very awkward minutes until Evelyn arrived. She did the necessary introductions, but I couldn't wait to excuse myself, leaving them for a family chat!

A few days later I was met at the Lagos docks by Tom McGhee, the ICI accountant, who took me to my new flat, and invited me to dinner at his house the following evening. When I turned up, there were two other couples and a solo man. Sometime during dinner, after a glass or two of wine, Tom asked me how the voyage had gone and had there been any shipboard romance for me. Not wishing to sound too dull, I said something like, "Oh yes, I met a pretty girl from Paisley, and we had a great time together." Oh no! It turned out that the man on his own was on his own because his little Scottish wife, who had just sailed from Liverpool with their new baby, was too tired to accompany her husband to dinner that evening. Once again I excused myself as soon as I could.

CHAPTER FIVE

There were two brand-new flats on the first floor of the building where I was to live. Mine was large with two bedrooms and all mod cons. The other, quite similar, was occupied by a rather older person, who told me he was the manager of a small trading company based in the city. He said he was awaiting the arrival of a new employee with whom he was going to share his flat. He didn't tell me who it was, so imagine my dismay when I opened my front door the next day to find Peter Kent standing there. I had largely avoided him on the boat, and hadn't particularly taken to him, with his loud voice, which seemed to rise above everyone else's wherever he was. Now there he was, holding out his hand and asking if he could come in for a quick word.

What he wanted to ask me was, rather than staying in his manager's spare room, could he live with me, on the understanding that we would share all expenses. Well, that would be a pretty good deal for him, because there weren't any expenses. ICI paid the rent, electricity, rates, everything except food and drink. I wasn't sure what my new employers would say if they found out. However, I couldn't help feeling a bit sorry for Peter who was being very friendly and I reckoned I could do with the company, so I agreed that he could move in that evening. Thus began a deep and lasting friendship, which continues to this day, between me and the man I always call my best friend – although, like all best friends, we do exasperate each other from time to time!

With Peter and a beach boy

My job was fascinating. There was almost no limit to the industrial products ICI sold in that market. Little by little I learned about the availability of a long list of chemicals and their applications, plus the better-known products like Dulux, Perspex, PVC for plastic goods and sandals, leathercloth for cars and furniture, and all the products of the dyestuffs division. We sold Terylene for fishing nets, polythene film, sulphuric acid for batteries, hydrated lime for road building, fertilisers and insecticides; in fact, the whole range except for pharmaceuticals for which I was not qualified. There were so many products that there was no excuse for not selling something wherever I went.

On one of my early sales tours with car and driver, for instance, I visited big factories which produced huge quantities of woven cotton fabric, in order to sell them expensive dyes, especially jade green, the national colour, which was used for almost everything, from flags to school uniforms. If, as often happened, the factory manager had just done a deal with a German or Swiss company, I was then expected to sell him something else. Didn't their factory need a coat of paint? If it was dim inside, how about some corrugated Perspex in the roof to let in some daylight? Or maybe some caustic soda for their bleaching process or even weed killer for their car park? There was no end to it, and after each trip, sometimes two weeks and a thousand miles long, I had to present a sheaf of visit reports, each one accompanied by a substantial number of orders to justify my existence. It was tough, often staying in the most basic 'rest houses', deep in the bush, with next to no facilities, but I loved it, and made friends of many nationalities all over the north of that amazing country.

During the first weeks there was a flurry of letters, I might even call them love letters, between B and me. In spite of our 'sensible' arrangement, we were missing each other badly, and this came over loud and clear in our writings. Neither of us could see any point in being sensible for fifteen long months, and, early in my tour though it was,

I began to wonder whether the company might make an exception to their rule.

Summoning up courage, I approached the general manager, whom I had only met twice, explained how I felt, and formally requested his permission to marry B. He was a real gentleman, saying there and then that, while he would have to check with head office in London, he saw no serious difficulty. Confirmation arrived a day or two later and I took time off to make a personal and confidential international call in the office of Cable and Wireless in the noisy centre of Lagos.

Poor B. Above the din of the traffic outside and interference on the line, I could hardly hear myself speak. At first she didn't even know who it was, but eventually, when I had shouted, "WILL YOU MARRY ME!" three times, she whispered a tearful, "Yes" – which I did *just* hear.

Everything was arranged for a full-scale (except I only had a lounge suit!) white wedding in the main Church of England by Lagos racecourse on 19 May 1959. Both B and her mother had been brought up as Roman Catholics, but between them they had decided that, if she was to have children with me, they should be christened and brought up in the C of E.

Three days before the ceremony, I drove out to Lagos Airport to meet them. They were to be accommodated in the house of Bill Sykes, the assistant general manager and his wife, who made them very welcome and comfortable. B was more stunning than ever and I took enormous pride in introducing her around, especially to Peter, of course!

He was to be my best man and had got some of my closest friends together for a stag night.

First, we all went for several drinks at the Club, followed by dinner, more drinks at a night club called Mogambo, and continued on from there. Now Peter is not always truthful and is given to exaggeration, but he does say we all finished up in a local open-air joint called the Lido, where we had more to drink and danced the night away very closely with some of the local ladies.

All I remembered was that I was in really bad shape when I woke on my wedding day, especially when Peter and I climbed into the company's Ford Prefect, to find that it was stuck fast in mud. However much the wheels spun and however hard we pushed, it could not be persuaded to take us to the church. We did however get a lift and, mud bespattered as we were, just made it before B. She had lost her father many years before, and Bill Sykes had agreed to give her away.

Isn't she lovely!

B was an absolute vision in the white A-line dress which had been found for her in Dickins and Jones in the short time available. We still have flowers from her bouquet, but sadly at some time lost the tape recording, which was made on an old-fashioned Grundig recorder, concealed in the pulpit. To tell the truth it was no great loss, because any promises we made standing before that altar were drowned out by the heavy rain thundering on the corrugated iron roof of the church and a crowd of several thousand punters cheering their favourite horses at the racecourse across the road!

After a reception hosted by the general manager and his wife on the lawn of their mansion, we said goodbye to B's sweet and lovely mother, who was to stay on for a few days, and thanked all those who had been so wonderful to us. Poor Peter, having performed his duties and excellent speech to perfection, had to make other arrangements for his accommodation, because we were off. Where did we go? To the airport to fly to Accra, capital of Ghana.

Only a few months before, the company had opened up a small office and factory in Tema, twenty miles outside Accra, which would make and sell a popular insecticide used to protect the vital cocoa crop from a particular bug which ate nearly half of it. Although a manager was already there, he needed an assistant to help him with sales of other ICI products throughout that exciting young country, which had been recently led to independence by Dr Kwame Nkrumah.

We honeymooned for a week in the newly completed Ambassador Hotel. It had been opened the week before with a grand dinner attended by the president himself and was looking splendid throughout. During our stay we discovered that this was only after a major clean up in the great ballroom. Apparently it had been decided to follow Nkrumah's big speech with the serving of a really special dessert to celebrate the occasion. This was crêpes Suzette, which involved the setting alight of brandy, already poured over a hundred individual little pans held by the waiters. Very unfortunately, this was too much for the automatic sprinkler system, which immediately covered everyone – including the president – and everything with white foam. Hence the clean up, which had been completed just in time for our honeymoon!

Having borne most of the cost of our wedding and our subsequent transfer, ICI also picked up the hotel bill, so it was two happy people who finally arrived in Tema, where another brand-new flat awaited us. Tema was a recently constructed town, built to serve the almost completed new harbour. This was to take over from Accra's surf port, which for centuries had received goods from all over the world by the use of canoes whose crews fought their way out through huge surf to waiting freighters. Having loaded up, each one would return much more quickly on the crest of a wave laden with foodstuffs, cement, fertiliser or one of many other essentials. Occasionally, in order to carry a car ashore they would strap two canoes together with planks in between, making a sort of catamaran. The vehicle, usually brand new, would then be lowered from the ship onto the heaving vessel for the 500-yard journey ashore. It was a fantastic sight to see the speed with which they reached the beach, although I have to say that the trip wasn't always successful. There is said to be more than one Rolls Royce lying on that seabed, destined never to glide along the palm-lined avenues of Accra!

Arriving at the hottest time of year, we were relieved to find air conditioners in the office and in the flat. Not all employers provided this luxury, and it made a big difference. I did miss it when I set off on tour for a week or so, selling my wares. Again I had to rely on poorly equipped rest houses, which were manned by a willing manager. Usually he had a phone, and I would be able to book ahead, to find him running out to meet me. Thereafter, he would do absolutely everything for me, including cleaning, food, drink, even a little hot shaving water, and I always gave him a good tip on departure.

The job was much the same as in Nigeria, except that the distances were not so great. For this reason, I only had a smaller car and usually went without a driver. While the product from our factory needed no selling because it was purchased in bulk by the government, there was the same ready market for everything else I had to sell. In fact, demand built up to such a degree that we started holding certain stock in a warehouse on the factory site. Things like paint, sulphuric acid or, for instance, copper pipes for plumbing, were much easier to sell in that way, rather than telling a potential customer that, while we would be happy to supply him, he would have to wait six weeks while his requirements came across the sea from England!

Entirely different were my visits to certain potential customers in the capital itself. For example, we would see a notice in the paper announcing that the Ministry of Agriculture was seeking quotations for, perhaps, 6,000 tons of fertiliser. This meant that I would have to visit the ministry in Accra urgently, all dressed up in jacket and tie, in order to collect the forms and notify the officer concerned that we at ICI were interested in supplying. There followed urgent cables between us and the manufacturing division in England in order to extract the best price and delivery. Often we got the order, but by no means always.

Sometimes I would hear that a large factory or warehouse of some sort was being designed by a well-known architect. Again without delay, I would make an appointment to persuade him that corrugated Perspex should be specified for the builder to use in the roof to allow sufficient daylight to enter. If I was successful, this would mean that, when the time came, the chosen contractor would have to place a big order with me worth perhaps £10,000, which our plastics division back in Welwyn Garden City would be pleased to supply. I was especially interested to visit several gold mines (which had given the country its original pre-independence name of the Gold Coast) in the Ashanti region to negotiate for the supply of the chemicals they required for the extraction of gold from the ore.

B and I made several really good friends, and often went as a group to the Tema Beach Club. It was not much more than a shack on the beach, I suppose, but the fresh fish was delicious, there was shelter from the sun and membership was supposed to be exclusive. Not always though. A couple of times we were there at the same time as the president of Ghana, and I don't think for a moment that he was a paid-up member!

By this time B was pregnant and we started to go with a picnic to one of the lovely palm-fringed beaches, which were both nearer to home and calmer than the beach club. We were enjoying ourselves one Sunday on our favourite one (until they put a 5-foot sewage pipe across it the following year!) called Paradise Beach, when B announced that she'd better go into hospital, because things were starting to happen. We left quickly and made it in plenty of time. I didn't actually attend Andrew's birth but received a call from the matron early the next morning, to say that he had been born. Tearing up to the hospital, I was running from the car in the direction of the ward when I passed a nurse who was well known to me from prenatal visits. "Is everything all right?" I shouted, not slowing down one bit. "Yes," she answered. "He's fine, except he's got two heads!" Maybe she thought it was funny, but it gave me a very scary moment before I crashed into B's room to find mother and baby both fine.

We hardly had time to wet the baby's head because two days later we were to hold the 'official' opening of the insecticide factory, with the president himself cutting the tape. Refreshments were laid on, the press all arrived and, an hour late, Nkrumah's motorcade drove in. I was one of the welcoming party, and imagine my excitement when, having shaken hands with the great man, I was introduced to an even greater visitor whom he had brought along for the occasion – Haile Selassie, no less, 'Lion of Judah'! Small in stature he may have been, but as his piercing eyes met mine some kind of thrill ran through me.

* * *

We became increasingly fond of our life in West Africa. As well as sharing responsibility for the factory, I was given an even wider range of the company's products to sell, and in travelling along the coast to Takoradi or up to the Saharan border I became really fond of its colourful people, their culture and especially their Highlife music.

Dressed Ghanaian fashion

We bought several lengths of their bright and intricately woven Kente cloth and were proud owners of a genuine Ashanti stool. These were a special shape, concave for comfort and only recognised as the real thing if they were carved out from a single, large chunk of teak. They were usually only possessed by the local chief, but occasionally, far out in the countryside, an expert carver could be persuaded to part with one, in exchange for a tidy sum (about £15).

There was only one thing that spoiled that first tour in Ghana and it came in the person of Mr Arthur, the man I had recruited as factory manager. He started off fine, giving me great support in the new enterprise and gaining considerable respect from his subordinates. I even remember him giving his personal help to one of them who was suffering from the effects of a tapeworm. The head of the disgusting thing had been exposed by an incision in the man's skin, but then it had to be drawn out. This was done by fixing the head to a smooth piece of wood, which then had to be turned every day, rather like a fishing line or a kite string. It was Mr Arthur who did this for the man every morning. It wasn't painful but it was essential not to miss a single day, and one morning after nearly a month, Mr Arthur told me that the whole worm had come out.

Even as I congratulated him on his persistence with the worm, I noticed a change in him. There were red streaks in his eyes, his speech was slurred, and on his breath I couldn't help noticing the sweet smell of palm wine, the local hooch. Over the following week, as these symptoms increased, and his condition began to affect his time keeping, his work and even the courtesy which he had always accorded me, I felt I had to do something.

Private chats and even warnings were to no avail, and there came a time when I had to give him his notice in writing. On reading this, the man lost all reason, threatening me in such a vicious way that I had to call for help. Still he went on and became so mad that he had to be removed from the site by force. As he was bundled into the company van, he calmed down for a moment and turned his drunken eyes on me. Making a well-known five-fingered West African gesture with his right hand he then laid a curse on me, which, he solemnly declared, would stay with me for the rest of my days. As he was driven off, I wondered whether the booze had turned him into some kind of a witch doctor. Either way, I never saw him again, and touch wood, I have lived to a ripe old age without his crazy image or 'juju' troubling me in my sleep!

In June 1960, our first home leave came along. With the rules of import duty as they were, we took full advantage and ordered a brand-new white Peugeot 404, duty free, to be collected in Milan. In this way, with special red number plates, we were able to drive it round Europe on a touring holiday, and back to England for the remaining six weeks of our leave.

Finally, we could ship it to West Africa, where we could either sell it at a profit or use it as our personal car (much smarter than the Ford Prefect provided by the company).

When we wrote to my parents about our plans, my brave mother did not hesitate. She would fly to meet us in Rome, where we would introduce her to her new grandson, by then eight months old. After a few days together, she would then take him home, while we had a couple of weeks to collect the car and tour the continent on our own.

Well, although we could not be sure how it would work out, it sounded good, and the four of us duly met up in a small Roman hotel. That night we all went out for a meal in a restaurant where we were offered a table outside. Andrew seemed to take to his granny. We had plenty to talk about and all went well until we began to be serenaded by a man with a guitar. He made a good sound, and I was reaching in my pocket for some change, when the most extraordinary thing happened. All of a sudden Phyl's right hand shot out like a chameleon's tongue. Before the musician could stop her, she seized the plectrum he was holding in his fingers. Dropping it in her handbag, she snapped it shut, telling him quite sharply and of course in English, "My other son plays the guitar, and he told me you should never use one of those things!"

Imagine the embarrassment! I could speak no Italian at all, and it was very difficult to placate the man, who was remonstrating so loudly in his native tongue, that many heads were beginning to turn in our direction. Phyl was adamant that my brother David knew best, but eventually I persuaded her to give it back wrapped in a much more valuable note than I had originally intended.

Poor Granny Porter. After we said goodbye at Rome airport, she had a pretty bad time, I'm afraid, with Andrew, whose favourite sport was kicking her ankles at every available opportunity. Although she never did admit it, I reckon she was pretty glad to hand him over when we eventually arrived home in our smart car, and took him off her hands.

* * *

ICI must have been reasonably happy with my performance, because the next time they wanted to open a new office, this time in Kano, Northern Nigeria (where I had landed in my sticky hot uniform four years earlier) they again sent for me. This was first mooted around Easter 1962, the idea being to spend a few months in Lagos familiarising myself with the fast-growing market and going on a couple of courses. In the meantime, a new house was being built for us in Kano, specially designed, with a small office in the back, cooled by a huge air conditioner.

This suited us fine because B was pregnant again, with the new baby expected in July. We decided that rather than putting her into one of the not very nice city hospitals, she would have her new baby at our temporary home in Lagos. The trouble was that we didn't have the time to get to know the midwife very well, as we had in Tema, nor indeed the doctor who was always so busy. So it was that, again on a Sunday morning, when B went into labour, all was not so smooth. It took a long time to find the midwife, and by the time she had arrived, she said that the doctor should come quickly.

He did indeed come soon, but he had been at a Sunday curry party and was rather the worse for drink. By then, B was having a pretty bad time and he decided that she should be given 'twilight sleep'. This involved pouring a little chloroform onto a cotton pad, which was then put gently over her mouth and nose.

It worked for B in that it eased her, but it didn't go well for the doctor. He had decided that forceps were necessary, and as Julia began to appear, I saw him slip them into position either side of her tiny head. The trouble was that he had left the chloroform bottle balanced on the bed with no stopper, and all of a sudden, his elbow knocked it onto the floor, squirting neat chloroform in every direction.

That was the end of his participation. Whether it was the booze or the chloroform, or a mixture of both I shall never know, but he passed out on the floor. The midwife, who turned out to be a trainee, fled downstairs and into the garden gasping for breath.

Finding myself alone, I flung open all the windows and dunked my handkerchief in B's water jug. Holding it over my mouth and nose with my left hand I urged B to push harder. As she obeyed, I used my right hand to tighten the forceps together and give a gentle pull. Thus our Julia was born into my arms, and a couple of minutes later, the young midwife rushed in, to find me with a pair of the doctor's scissors, wondering where to cut the cord! Luckily, she took over then, and Julia finished up with a neat tummy button.

For months though, I did worry about her head, which had a squashed look about it!

There were of course, serious recriminations, but over fifty years on, lovely Julia has three beautiful daughters of her own. All I remember is the moment when I picked up that wet and rather bloody bundle and wondered where to put it!

* * *

The general manager was driven to the office each day in a prestige model of car called a Humber Super Snipe. Beautiful as it was, it was getting on a bit and on returning from leave in August 1962, he bought himself a brand-new Rover. Rather than selling the Humber to a poor second-hand market, it was decided to allocate it to me for all the mileage I was to do in the Northern Region.

Accordingly, we loaded up all our personal things plus the two children, ready for the nearly 600-mile trip to Kano. At the last minute Peter Kent asked if he could come with us, since he had business up there. By this time he had changed jobs and was selling a strange mixture of lines stretching from Pye records to Izal lavatory paper! Naturally I was glad to have my old friend along on this adventurous journey, and agreed readily. All went well as we reached the huge city of Ibadan and struck north through sparsely populated country towards Kaduna, the Northern Region's capital.

We decided we would stop for lunch at Jebba, a town famous for a statue and memorial to Mungo Park, the explorer who discovered the source of the Niger, but had unfortunately drowned in the rapids a few miles upstream. It proved to be unfortunate for us too, because, as we entered the outskirts of the town, the back axle of the old car packed up completely.

It was to be a major job, and I knew that the only chance of finding the part and a mechanic to fit it was three hours back in Ibadan. That is how I came to leave Peter with my pretty young wife and two children, with instructions to find a hotel for the night, while I got a lift in a 'mammy wagon', a colourful lorry full of people with their market purchases, going back the way we had come. On the front of the lorry in great silver letters, there was a sign, which read: IN GOD WE TRUST. How apt, I thought, as I waved everyone goodbye.

It was a nightmare twenty-four hours before I got back, but I did bring a mechanic and the part with me. The repair was completed, and in due course we reached our new home in Kano, over three days after we had set out. I reported by telephone to my immediate superior in Lagos, who quickly acquired authority for me to buy a new Vauxhall, which was to carry me thousands of miles around that huge territory.

From Sokoto across to Maiduguri, from Katsina down to Ilorin, it measured nearly 250,000 square miles, which made it necessary for me to have a full-time driver. We also had a cook/steward, wash boy, nanny, garden boy and a night watch (for some reason called a watch night). The company paid them all except the nanny. In due course, as we shall see, there were also two horse boys, but they too were down to us.

Our new bungalow, which was still being painted on our arrival, was completely surrounded by groundnut and cassava fields, except for the front, where we had a driveway which skirted a lawn, complete with a large mango tree. Beyond that, the other side of a narrow, dusty lane, and hardly a hundred yards away, ran the railway line to the northern border. This alarmed us at first until we found that there was only one train each way each week. Furthermore, its dozen or so carriages were drawn only very slowly by a proper steam engine, which gave the children (and us!) a big thrill as it chuffed by.

I soon furnished my little office and engaged a young male secretary called Hyacinth, to do my typing and take calls when I was away on tour. My bosses were in Lagos, a two-hour flight away and I loved it!

Apart from the ever-growing range of industrial products I had to sell, I had new and challenging duties concerning Indigo Vat Dyestuff. For centuries, the Tuareg people of the Sahara Desert, which lay only two hours' drive to the north, had harvested the dark blue vegetable dye, in which to dip their robes and turbans. The habit had spread south to the Nigerian Emirs and their subjects. They had learned that, if they folded and folded the dark blue finished fabric about 10 times, and beat the resultant little pile with wooden mallets, it would shine in the sun like bronze. It was also supposed to keep mosquitos away!

For this purpose, the root of the indigo plant was highly valued, but, when mixed with water, it was not really very strong. So when, some years before our arrival, ICI and other chemical companies started offering a synthetic indigo dye with all the same properties but twenty times the strength, it was snapped up by those who made their living dyeing cloth.

Every town and village had an area given over to a number of 12-foot deep holes into which they put water and indigo plus salt and camel dung for 'fixing' the dye. ICI's concentrated Lion brand came in tiny quarter-pound tins, which retailed at a little over a pound each. It was an enormous market with total tonnage exceeding 1,500 tons per annum, and everyone wanted their share. To avoid cut-throat competition, the price paid by the five trading companies who imported it from Europe and the price at which the latter sold it locally, were agreed each year. This agreement, which was kept secret, was signed by all concerned including the three main manufacturers back in Europe: ICI, BASF (Germany) and CIBA (Switzerland). It was a pretty dodgy practice and wouldn't be allowed these days, but it was designed to maintain a decent profit.

It hadn't lasted though, with the 'rules' being broken and undercutting taking place on all sides in spite of the annual agreement. As the price plummeted, the only people who benefited were the ultimate users in the villages, and the big producers in Europe weren't going to have this. A special meeting was convened in London, at which, once again, all sorts of promises were made. Unfortunately, as everyone knew, such undertakings were made to be broken, especially when those on the ground in Nigeria could not be policed. Oh yes they could, said ICI, and sent for Porter!

So that was one of my main jobs, to establish who was selling the product at what price and to send a stream of detailed reports to head office. I would visit the dye pits, especially those in Kano itself, asking the dyers (in Hausa at which, since army days, I was still proficient), if I could see their tins. The subsequent conversation normally revealed their source and the price they had paid. The arrangement was that, if any producer or importer were constantly named as a price cutter in my reports, that company's quota would be reduced at the next meeting. I am not convinced that it worked, but I suppose I did succeed to some extent in putting on the brake, and the contributions from the suppliers paid most of the expenses of my family and me.

Back in the house, B was doing a great job turning it into a home, showing Musa, the cook steward, how she liked things done, and buying plants, like canna lillies and bougainvillea for Shehu to plant. He was our devoted gardener, who had suffered from leprosy, but it was under control and he didn't let it bother him. After a slightly anxious time, we learnt that we shouldn't either.

We persuaded the Lagos head office to order some fairly expensive furniture, manufactured by a Danish company down there, to be sent up to us. It was made of oiled teak and looked great. The only trouble was that every year during the harvest time, there came a strong, constant and very dry wind, called the harmattan. As it blew remorselessly from the desert for two months, everything, *everything*, dried out. There was dust everywhere – even our lips cracked and so did our smart new furniture in spite of its regular teak oiling. We could be sitting down with perhaps a beer on a side table when, without warning, there would be a sound like a pistol shot and the table would split from side to side. When the general manager paid his first visit to see how we were getting on, he was not pleased!

B's hands were full, first finding a little school for Andrew, who needed taking and collecting every day and then spending lots of time in the hospital with Julia. She had been born with both feet turned slightly inwards (not my fault!) and the poor little thing spent four hot months with both legs in plaster. It gave her and her mother all sorts of problems, but thank goodness for those wonderful doctors in faraway Africa, because she grew out of it completely. She has recently done a half-marathon and skis nearly as fast as her three speeding daughters!

We met every day at lunchtime in the sunshine at the club, where there was a large pool. Andrew loved it and swam like a fish. It was good for me to get out of my air-conditioned office for a salad and a swim. There were usually quite a few pretty young mums there but apart from me, only one man. He was an English bachelor, manager of one of the banks, always sitting in one corner with a newspaper and a beer. Nobody took much notice of him, but I saw one day that he had torn a hole in his newspaper so that he could admire the women in their swimsuits without being seen!

After noticing this on several occasions, it was clear to me that he made a practice of this, but I never did let on. After all he wasn't my bank manager!

* * *

Then we bought two horses. Neither of us had ridden before but we had friends who loved it, and one of them talked me into buying a plain brown nag who we called Teapot. He was really stubborn, apparently aware that the body on his back had no idea how to persuade him against his will to follow the path for two or three miles out into the countryside. With a lot of pulling and pushing from my friends on their fancy mounts, I eventually persuaded him after a week or so to venture out. The trouble came when we turned back, as the scrawny beast sensed that his oats were awaiting him at the stables. Without a care for any bush, tree, low branch, person or other horse, and with me hanging on for dear life, he bolted for home, and only stopped when he saw his horse boy standing by his stable with a handful of corn. Thank goodness he was persuaded not to go in to that low mud structure or I would have been literally scraped off his back.

I soon changed him for a much bigger beast, who having been schooled to a reasonable degree, was much easier to control.

Then B fell in love with another one. Jet black, sleek and shiny with a flowing mane, he was called Takobi (Hausa for 'sword'). She just had to have him and became skilled in the saddle. She even got the horse boys to teach the children. Never having been taught, I don't think either of us

Andrew and Julia riding lessons

were very pretty riders, but we joined in with the others, especially on early Sunday morning rides and paper chases along river beds. On our return before breakfast, there was a tradition that a large silver polo trophy would be filled with brandy and ginger ale to be passed round till it was empty. We were usually very thirsty from our exertion and on occasion that big cup was refilled more than once. Typical of the expatriate community in the sixties!

One particular Sunday, becoming bored by the slow canter at which we all were proceeding through the countryside, I went ahead and hid behind a large bush. Once the others had passed, I waited a bit, then galloped up behind them, spurring my new steed, as I had by then learnt to do, and uttering a cry worthy of the wildest cowboy.

My friends were not amused, as the morning peace was shattered and a couple of the horses reared up in surprise.

One Irishman, an experienced horseman and a vet to boot, was particularly upset and said angrily, "Tony, if you want to behave like that on a horse, you'd better get it out of your system and take up polo!"

So that's what I did, and it became the centre of my sporting life for the rest of our time in West Africa. As I became more and more keen, I increasingly spent money on well-schooled Arab ponies, saddles and other tack, not to mention two horse boys, three stables and literally tons of corn, plus expensive supplements to make the ponies go faster than ever.

Polo can be a dangerous game. Imagine two horses and riders, together weighing nearly a ton, racing towards each other at a combined speed of 60 mph to get to the ball first. A head-on collision could be fatal, so there have to be rules, very strict ones. They can be complicated and difficult at first. For example, if the riders are at right angles to each other, both going for the ball, who gives way?

But I got used to these rules as they began to make sense (except perhaps for the annoying one which allows a player to hook another's stick from behind, just when he's about to strike the ball!). There is a handicap system, which requires a new player to start at zero goals. If, after his first game, he is deemed bad enough, which he usually is, he then goes down to minus 2 goals, the lowest handicap in the game. This is what happened to me, but over the years I did improve and climbed back up through zero to a plus 2. This was quite respectable, though, I have to admit, the best handicap a player can have is plus 10 (there are less than 10 of these in the whole world!).

After a game

I made the Kano team, and we toured all over the Northern Region having a great time and occasionally bringing home a trophy. Easily the most important tournament was held in Kaduna (the provincial capital) every year and as it approached in 1964, I splashed out and bought a big black powerful stallion, worthy of such an occasion. The scene was set for our match, with crash barriers all round to keep the crowds back. As I was ready before the other three members of our team I came out with stick and ball for a little practice. The impatient crowd gave a little cheer every time I connected, and I couldn't resist having a long

B on Takobi

Polo Programme – Capital of Northern Nigeria

Beating to Windward

Zandra Rhodes for Autumn 1975
British Fashion Week

Number 5 Queen Anne's Gardens sold to buy the island

Burgh Island Next Stop – (Photo Credit Mark Grimshaw)

Stately Arrival

Aveton Gifford Classic Car Show – (Photo Credit Mark Grimshaw)

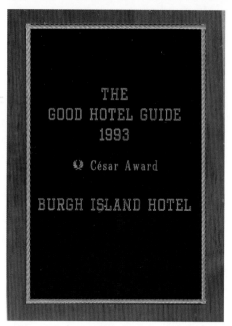

*For recreating with panache the high life of
the Twenties – 1993 award*

*Piccadilly sign,
arranged free by hotel guest*

Three cottages into one Brittany

Hannah's Go-kart

Susie's Sunflower 2008

shot at goal. It wasn't hard enough though, and the ball was dribbling to stop short to the right of the goal. Determined not to allow this (and probably showing off a bit too!) I galloped after it and scored with a neat under the neck shot.

I got my cheer all right, but unfortunately I had too much momentum. That horse wasn't made for jumping and skidded to a halt just before hitting the crash barrier behind the goal, but I carried on between his ears, over the barrier and through the crowd, landing on my head. Of course I wore a helmet, which helped, but something had happened to my neck and I lay still.

I missed the rest of that match (served me right!) as I was stretchered off to hospital. It was there that I was informed that technically I had a broken neck. Horrified at the news and in some pain, I was then told that it could be cured with traction. This involved sitting on a bed and having a harness put under my chin and stretched over my head. The doctor then wound a handle connected to a rope, which pulled the harness and my head upwards towards the ceiling. "Shout stop when you can't take it any more," he said, and I was very brave. In the end, though, I did call out, because I thought my head would come off otherwise. That was when he went round to the back, where there was another handle, lowered the bed an inch or two in order to stretch my neck that little bit more, and left the room.

It sounded crazy at the time, but it worked. No longer did I have a technically broken neck and I played in the tournament the next day! We were knocked out in the semi-final.

The Kano team 1964

I have never played polo back in England. Far too expensive. However, as a grandpa, I have entertained children from time to time, perched astride a chair turned backwards with a broom, demonstrating the shots. They love it when I show them, with an imaginary ball. Forward forehand, forward backhand, backward backhand, backward forehand, under the neck forehand, under the neck backhand, under the tail forehand, under the tail backhand. Then there are two shots which I never used involving hitting the ball between the horse's legs. There is a serious risk of laming him, and both these shots are called, for obvious reasons, the millionaire's shot!

CHAPTER SIX

All this time B loved riding, especially her morning hack. Her doki (horse) boy would arrive at the house with the gleaming black Takobi after breakfast and she would canter for an hour or more in the countryside that surrounded us.

She was never tempted to play polo, although she often came to cheer me on. It was at one of these matches that a ladies race was proposed, and B agreed to take part. It took place at the end of the next race day at the Kano course, with five entrants, over the flat. These ladies didn't do jumps!

In that race, B rode a beautiful Palomino, owned by a wealthy local businessman. She came a creditable second, and perhaps it should have been left at that. Later, though, there was another race, in which, at my suggestion, she agreed to ride my tall fierce black arab. Round the final bend, she was just in the lead and we were all on our feet urging her on when she collided with a challenging horse. To our horror, she fell, finishing up motionless on the ground right in front of the grandstand. Try as I might, I couldn't get to her through the crowd, but there were first-aid people who quickly resuscitated her, and helped her up into the stand where I was blocked in.

There was apparently no lasting damage, but I did become concerned when, a couple of weeks later, we found that she was two months pregnant with our third child. Again, I need not have worried, as her pregnancy proceeded normally, and we began to make plans for the birth. We knew of a Catholic mission hospital in Jos, a hill station with a cool climate, set on a high plateau, 150 miles to the east, and made an appointment to go there with the children. Being very happy after a visit to meet the doctor and his staff, we booked B in for the end of December 1964, and looked forward to the happy occasion with confidence. In the meantime, setting horses and babies to one side, I thought it was about time for me to turn to the work that I was paid to do.

One of the hundreds of products I had to sell did hold a special interest for me, because it potentially had the power to ensure a constant supply of food for the huge number of people who lived in the northern province. Called Gammalin A, it was a perfectly safe insecticide, which killed weevils.

It worked like this. At harvest time, farmers would cut their corn by hand and store it, not as threshed grain, but 'on the head' in tiny mud huts called 'rumbus'. There it would stay for up to six months, when the corn heads would be removed, one by one, to be threshed, so that the dry grain would fall off, ready for the cooking process.

The trouble was that, during that long storage process, hungry weevils got to work, consuming between 30 and 50% of the precious grain. Over the years, various methods of protection had been tried, but were found to be ineffective or dangerous. This last included spraying the growing crops with insecticides like DDT, but this was poisonous and could cause serious harm if consumed by humans, even in tiny quantities.

Following detailed and exhaustive trials, Plant Protection Ltd, a fully owned ICI company back in England, had developed a safe alternative, which entailed sprinkling a powder based on kaolin (china clay). The idea was to spread a small amount of the powder (it turned out to be one and half match boxes full) on each layer as they were piled up in the rumbu, which was then closed.

The powder consisted of 99.5% kaolin and 0.5% BHC (benzene hexachloride), the active ingredient which killed the weevils during storage. When each head was removed and beaten to separate the grain, which was then winnowed in the wind, very nearly all the powder was removed, leaving only an infinitesimal amount, which by then contained hardly any BHC. Even this disappeared when the grain was pummelled with a pestle and mortar into a paste, and finally boiled in water before consumption.

Once the product had passed the most stringent safety tests, ten little bags, each weighing two pounds, were sent out to me in Kano, so that I could arrange field trials. I had already approached five different farmers, giving them an idea of the safety and benefits, and offering a free supply for the 1964 season, if they would cooperate in the trial on their crop.

They were necessarily spread far and wide over Northern Nigeria, which meant hundreds of miles driving (I still had a driver) as the trials were laid down and later monitored. That year they proved to be an unqualified success, with those five farmers being amazed as the corn was in the same condition on removal as it had been when placed in their rumbus, months before.

That was only the beginning. For the following three years I toured the whole of that huge area introducing Gammalin A to government agricultural officers, who in turn demonstrated it to farmers, and our sales grew to nearly two hundred tons, all in 2 lb bags!

That was when the fun really started for me. It did seem crazy that this heavy stuff was being shipped from London to Lagos, then over 500 miles north to Kano, when 99.5% of it consisted of clay which was available under the ground in most parts of the world. If a suitable deposit could be found somewhere in the northern area, where the product was mostly needed for their corn, only 0.5% BHC would have to be shipped out all that way. A small mixing/grinding factory would do the rest.

Since, by this time, I knew the territory, its inhabitants and their language, I was charged with the task of discovering whether a deposit of suitable clay existed somewhere within a hundred miles of Kano, where the factory could be built.

Happy as I was to seek it out, often on the way to established industrial customers, it was no easy job. By this time

Gammalin A in its original form had built up a loyal following amongst the farmers, but they would have been suspicious of any product which appeared even slightly different. This meant that any clay I found would have to be pure white with exactly the same alkalinity and density as the Cornish kaolin used in the English factory. Little did I know how difficult this would be as more and more samples I airmailed to Plant Protection were rejected for one or more reasons.

I was actually quite surprised to find how often my enquiries revealed small mines, often in the middle of nowhere, which supplied clay for a variety of purposes, including cheap whitewash, road markings, paint, and so on. For six months I followed every clue, visiting holes in the ground and mines of all sizes. By this time I had persuaded the company to buy me a big front-wheel-drive Citroen DS23. It had adjustable suspension and on the top notch, one inch more clearance than a Land Rover, just the thing for dust roads with big humps in the middle often concealing dangerous rocks! Even so, there were times when I parked this wonderful machine to continue the search for my precious sample by foot, bicycle and even horseback!

One of the obvious places to look was in Plateau Province. It consisted of rocky terrain, just the sort of ground where I had learnt that kaolin deposits were most likely to be found. Furthermore, it would suit me to be in that area the last week of December 1964, when B was due in hospital in Jos, the provincial capital, for the birth of our third child.

Accordingly, all four of us set off in our fine new Citroen a few days after Christmas and checked into the long-established and comfortable Jos hill station, to await the great event. The trouble was it didn't happen when it should have happened, and with the doctor saying it would still be some days, it was agreed that I would take Andrew and Julia back to Kano to spend the New Year holiday with friends. This I did, returning to Jos without delay. When I found B still waiting, I told her that I really should get on with my hunt. The next day I gave my driver the day off, so that he could visit relatives, and set off on my own in search of my precious kaolin for just one day.

Very unfortunately, when I was nearly a hundred miles from Jos, driving along a deserted track on the plain beneath the plateau, my faithful Citroen let me down – literally. One of the pipes, through which passed the precious suspension fluid, fractured and the whole car sank down comfortably in the deep sand. I always carried water and had a sandwich or two left over from lunch, but all I could do was to stay where I was for the night. The next day, I set out to walk, seeing only the odd herdsman until around midday I was picked up by the local English agricultural officer in his Land Rover. He took me to his home, where I hoped to call B, who I knew must have been wondering. My saviour had a battery-powered radio telephone – but it was flat. It took the rest of the day and most of the night to charge it with his little generator, so, by the time I got word to her, I had been missing for forty-eight hours. Poor thing, with the baby due any time, she had been really worried. But she kept calm and arranged for a mechanic to meet me at my car.

It got worse, because when I finally got back to her, she had received a message from my London head office contact, who knew nothing of all this, saying that I had to be back in Kano on 6 January to look after a main board director of ICI who was passing through. It was terrible for both of us, but I had to go again, driving slowly in the car, whose repair had only been botched by a local mechanic.

That night, hard to believe now, with the help of our cook Musa, I had to give a full-scale dinner party for this man and a few local dignitaries, and only got to bed around 2am. Little did I know at the time, but little Caroline was born while all this was going on, at 12.28am on 7 January. After all our careful advance planning, I was 150 miles away!

My friend Dieter, who was the Citroen agent, lent me his personal car, and I was in Jos again by mid-afternoon that same day to meet our new baby and my exhausted wife. All was well though, so the next morning I picked them both up from the hospital and headed home again.

I was probably going a bit too fast on that uneven road or, I have often thought, I should have had the suspension on the higher setting. Halfway home one of the drive shafts, connecting the gear box to the front wheel, hit a rock and the car stopped. I looked up and down the deserted road, and realised there was no help likely (oh for a mobile phone, unheard of in 1965!). With a newborn baby in the back, I decided that I should see if the car would move. I gingerly engaged gear, and was amazed to find that, although there was a quite loud clonk, the wheels actually turned. I tried again, and got the car moving slowly.

So, at a little under 20 mph we made the last seventy miles, arriving home in pitch dark. When, the next morning I returned the car to Dieter, he jacked it up to inspect the damage, and, while it was halfway up, the front offside wheel fell off! I looked at him in surprise, but he reminded me that those clever Citroens were designed to go on three wheels if the need arose.

* * *

It was so wonderful to be back with our new daughter and to introduce her to her big brother and sister. After all I'd been through, it was tempting to sit back for a few days. But I needed to keep head office in Lagos happy and was glad to report that, before my breakdown on that fateful day, I had found a very promising deposit of kaolin, a sample of which I rushed back to England.

Alas, after two weeks of tests I was again told by cable that it was too acidic, and I could have given up had it not been for a visit to a small village near Katsina in the north, where the dye pits used considerable quantities of our indigo. Taking a shortcut through the market, I saw a very old lady sitting cross-legged on the ground. In front of her lay a piece of cloth covered with little twists of newspaper. Curious, I asked her what they were for and she answered by passing one to me. Undoing it carefully, I found a small quantity of pure white powder, which she was selling for makeup.

Using my best Hausa, I succeeded in buying four little packets for a penny each and having thus made a friend of the woman, I felt able to ask her where she got the powder. She told me that she had bought it from a man on a donkey who passed by very early every Wednesday morning.

Fortunately, the village was only about eighty miles from home, so, having set out in darkness, I was there to intercept the donkey man the following Wednesday. He was very suspicious when I asked him where he got his clay, about half a hundredweight of which was strapped to either side of his donkey. In due course though, by dint of a certain amount of flattery and silver in his palm, he gave me directions.

Fortune favoured me, for the place to which he had directed me and where I found the mine belonged to the Emir (chief) of Katsina with whose son I played polo from time to time. This meant that when my sample was at last proclaimed perfect by Plant Protection in England I could easily negotiate with the owner, and a deal was struck. Previously designed plans were put into action and less than a year later we opened a small factory capable of producing hundreds of tons of safe insecticide per year. It was gleaming white in a locally produced little bag, identical with the original, and less than a quarter of the price to farmers. To the best of my knowledge, locally made Gammalin A is still being sold and saving lives fifty years on.

With no immediate neighbours, and living in a house at the end of a sandy cul-de-sac, I used to worry about security,

131

especially when I was away for more than a week. We had our donkey, a parrot, our spaniel Charlie, and, of course, our 'watch night' – but we still had scares.

Although the house had air conditioners, we didn't use them in January and February when the cold harmattan wind blew, so we left the windows in the bedrooms open at night. Security was provided by a three-inch mesh screen made of steel. We thought that was good enough, but one night, being woken by a slight noise, I looked up in the dim light and saw my trousers high up and floating towards the window! When I jumped out of bed with a shout, B asked me what was the matter, and as I pointed, we both saw the trousers fall to the floor. When I switched on the light, there was a long cane, which a thief had been using as a fishing rod, sticking it through the mesh covering the window. I supposed the man guessed that if he got the garment near enough to the mesh, he might be able to riffle the pockets for money.

Quickly dressing, I ran out, past the sleeping Charlie, to where the watch night ('Maigardi' in Hausa) normally sat under the mango tree between patrols of the garden. At least, that was the idea, but he too was fast asleep with his sword by his side. "Maigardi! Maigardi! Wake up!" I yelled, then asked him if he had seen anyone. He told me that a little while ago, a man had asked him the time. I gave him a serious ticking off, and told him that, if this happened again, he would be sacked (I hoped not because we were very fond of him).

Well, a couple of days later, as we arrived back late from the cinema, my headlights picked him out, slumped outside the front door. Stopping the car and walking quietly over, I bent over him to wake him up, ready to carry out my threat.

But no! This time the boot was on the other foot. As I stretched out my hand he suddenly sprang up and forced me against the wall, holding that flashing sword against my neck. Remonstrating, I was quickly released, but I had to admit it was one-all!

As well as riding, we had a great life, playing tennis, golf and joining the motor club. By the end of our four years in Kano, we had a big new Citroen DS Pallas, which was great for long rallies in soft sand and river beds. We also had a Mini Cooper, which we used for sprints and speed trials,

Our new Citroen

and even a little Citroën 2CV. This last was ideal for parking trials. Everyone else had to guess whether the odd wheel might be touching a white line, but we could remove all four doors and the boot and see the lines. We still have the trophies, in which we toasted all our victories at the time!

But all was not well with Nigeria. Tribal differences had always been known to surface from time to time. The Ibo people of the east did not always see eye to eye with the Yorubas of the west and neither of these largely Christian communities really got on with the massive Moslem population of the north. In 1966 the bubbling volcano erupted with the assassination of the Sardauna of Sokoto and the federal prime minster Tafewa Balewa, both leading Moslem figures.

This quickly escalated on the streets, with the deaths of many Ibo people who had made their homes and businesses in the North. Rosalind, our Ibo nanny, fled one night, and we were relieved to hear that she made it safely to her homeland. She was fortunate, but many were not, as the Hausa people took their revenge for the deaths of their leaders.

This was only the beginning. Colonel Ojukwu declared the Eastern Region independent and renamed it Biafra. The federal government was not having this and the bloody Biafran War ensued, with thousands dead and no apparent solution in sight.

Feeling vulnerable in our house stuck all by itself in a groundnut field alongside the railway, I took the precautionary step of sending the family home on early leave, while I decided what to do.

It was not safe to drive around the region, which my job still required of me, and there was no position for me in Lagos, so two months later head office advised me to close up the house and follow them home. Before leaving, I held a sale of our possessions which I couldn't easily take on the plane. I raised over 500 Nigerian pounds, which was to prove useful cash in our new predicament. I did get into serious trouble with B when she asked me what happened to her precious tennis racket and half a dozen books she had won as prizes at school, but was partially forgiven when the money reached England and was converted at a favourable rate to £700!

So, having passed the trumpeter on his camel, I found myself, for the second time in my life, climbing alone up the steps of an aircraft to fly away from West Africa, which had given me so much experience, fun and, oh yes, a wife and three children. As we took off, I could never have guessed how radically this journey and its destination were going to change the rest of my life.

Chapter Seven

During our leave in 1966, we had decided to get on the property ladder, and bought our first house. This is an easy date to remember, because, very soon after our completion, my parents came over from Sussex and together we watched England win the World Cup. For a four-bedroom family home with garage and garden in Alton, Hampshire, we paid £3,800. It was a good-looker: white with dark timbers. While it had been fun spending our leaves with parents, we did love having a few weeks in our very own house. We had, of course, a mortgage, the idea being to let it out while we were back in Nigeria. The sums worked out that, if we let it for £8 a week, one day it would be ours!

A carefully worded advert in the local paper produced several interested parties and, with our leave coming to an end, we chose a pleasant professional couple with excellent references from their bank and solicitor. A standing order was set up and we returned to Kano happy in the knowledge that all was well.

It wasn't. Within a week the couple cancelled the standing order, although we didn't know it until our statement a month later showed that nothing had been received from them. Airmail letters produced no reply, and since we had not used an agent, we had no way of knowing what was going on, or for that matter, even whether they were still there. After three blank months, we engaged the help of local solicitors, who established that the couple were indeed still in residence, but their legal letters about the outstanding debt remained unanswered as well.

As the weeks went by, we were having to pay the mortgage company from my wages in Kano. The long process of legal repossession ground on. A date was finally set for the court hearing. Sitting out in Africa, we awaited the result, hoping against hope that we would get rid of them and even be granted some money towards overdue rent and legal costs.

Wishful thinking! They didn't even turn up at the court, and when the bailiffs went round, they found the house deserted. No trace of them was ever discovered, and the glowing references proved to be forgeries. After eight months of rent-free living, we supposed they had moved to another part of the country to do the same to some other sucker. As for us, we had learnt our lesson and let the house through an agent for six months, with a month's notice either way, to a really nice Indian family. The rent was slightly more at £8.10 shillings (£8.50), but this extra bit was easily swallowed up by the agent's fees and of course the bills which had been mounting. As it turned out, with our unexpectedly early return from Nigeria, we did have to ask them to vacate a bit early, but it suited them and they went home to India soon afterwards.

At least we had somewhere to live, and unable to return to Kano, I was to be paid by ICI (Nigeria) Ltd for two months, at the end of which I was hoping to take up a position within the African department at headquarters in London. This was all very well but the pen-pushing job sounded very boring compared with what I had been doing; furthermore, without all the generous overseas allowances to which we had become accustomed, coupled with the cost of commuting every day, the pay was going to be inadequate. But it looked as if I had no choice.

Then, from absolutely nowhere, a choice did appear. B's sister, Barbara Hulanicki, had become a skilled fashion illustrator, and was in great demand. Through her link with Felicity Green, the fashion editor, she had conducted a highly successful editorial mail order venture in the *Daily Mirror* in 1964. During that time we had visited the flat in Cromwell Road, West London, from which she and her husband Fitz were dispatching thousands of little cotton gingham dresses each with a matching headscarf. It was very cheap and, having searched far and wide for more and more fabric, they succeeded in sending out nearly 17,000 sets, mostly manufactured by small factories in the East End of London. Subsequently, other offers were made under the name of Biba's Postal Boutique. This was the abbreviation of the name of her (and B's of course) younger sister who had been christened Biruta.

Consequently, Barbara opened a tiny boutique, also called Biba, in what had previously been a chemist's shop in Abingdon Villas, Kensington. With her brilliant eye and expert choice of colours and fabrics, she designed clothes that were to shake the fashion world. She and Fitz, who had by then left his job in advertising, put Biba on the map forever, as a result of huge international publicity and sheer hard work.

Eighteen months before I arrived back from Kano for the last time, they outgrew that little shop, and the London *Evening Standard* used big pictures of Biba's pretty sales girls running down Kensington High Street, pushing rails of Barbara's amazing little dresses on their way to the new and larger shop, two hundred yards up Kensington Church Street. This was typical of the brilliant ways that Barbara and Fitz got free publicity.

Manageress Eleanor Powell and the new shop
in Kensington Church St.
(Reproduced with the kind permission of the Antique Collectors' club)

High-fashion girls from all over London followed them to their new Biba Emporium, complete with its communal changing room and bentwood hat stands from which hung hats, feather boas plus, of course, the ever-changing inexpensive styles. On a busy Saturday morning, girls were to be seen literally fighting for their favourite item, as stocks sometimes sold out before lunch. Going back down Kensington Church Street, there would be an unending line of 'dolly birds', as Barbara called them, all carrying at least one of the coveted black-and-gold Biba bags. Unfortunately, though, not all of them had been paid for. The low lighting and communal changing room presented something of a haven for shop lifters, who became quite a problem, so much so that customers had to be limited to taking only a small number of items into the changing room to try on. There was always a danger that a girl who paid for a mini skirt might be wearing other items under her coat! The staff occasionally found a pile of strange used clothes in a corner of the changing room, where some young girl had changed into her chosen Biba outfit and walked out. Hundreds of girls came in every single week, and, if she was stopped, she could easily claim to have bought it the previous Saturday, and why on earth should she have the receipt on her? If it was a brand-new style, of course, she would have a problem.

With Biba clothes being featured constantly in national newspapers and magazines, not to mention local papers all over Britain, it was obvious that there was a huge demand out there that was not being satisfied. So Barbara and Fitz decided to go back to mail order.

Barbara's design skills did not finish with clothes and shops.

She worked with a really good company to produce the most beautiful catalogue, influenced throughout by her intricate knowledge of art deco and the 1930s. It bore no resemblance whatsoever to the thick telephone directory style catalogues being sent out by the large established mail order companies of the day. Printed on quality thick card and measuring nearly a foot high and six inches wide (to fit through letter boxes), when opened out it revealed the most stunning black-and-white or sepia photographs. Each one was veritably collectable, showing a pretty, slim girl with an oval face and huge eyes, wearing Biba. There were only two or three dozen items, including some of the accessories also for sale, but each was so beautifully displayed, with every detail so clear, that there was plenty from which to choose.

As this mouth-watering catalogue was being prepared to go to the printers, Fitz and Barbara knew there was still much to do. One thing was to build up the list of names to whom it would be sent. They placed a book by the till in the shop inviting customers to write their names and addresses or those of friends and relatives, who would like to receive a catalogue. At the same time, their PR people made it their business to get fashion writers featuring Biba in any way to encourage their readers to write in or phone for one. In these ways during the months leading up to the launch, many thousands of extra names were collected.

By this time, in addition to the photographic samples, cardboard patterns had been made and graded into three or four sizes. Fabrics had been ordered from suppliers who were expected to be capable of repeating quickly for the styles which proved the most popular. Essential items like buttons and zips were found, all to be dyed to match or to be covered in the various fabrics with which they would be used. Most importantly too, Barbara found a firm which could supply back neck labels, with her legendary Biba logo woven in gold on a black background. One of these was to be sewn into every garment.

So everything was in place, ready for the first catalogue to be launched in April 1968. But as the time approached, there was one important thing, or should I say person, who was decidedly not in place. When those thousands of catalogues were mailed out, and the orders started coming in, who was going to open the envelopes and check each order against the payment enclosed? Who was going to negotiate a good price with the manufacturer, get the necessary amount of fabric delivered, assemble the right number of buttons, zips and labels, draw up an order in the appropriate percentages of sizes and colours, all to be taken with the relevant set of patterns to factories on the other side of London? Who would arrange collection when they were ready, recruit staff to handle enquiries or complaints about quality or delays? Or count the money – cash, cheques and postal orders – and pay it into the bank deposit box, up to £5,000 a day, often late at night when everyone else had gone home? Rather late in the day, they started to look for such a person, and one evening Fitz took me for a drink to the Catherine Wheel pub, to ask me whether I might be interested. Coming out of the blue, his suggestion bowled me over. The best I could do was to ask a few questions and show interest, followed by a request for a little time to think about it. Fitz understood that it would be a big step for me to leave the mighty ICI to join a boutique, and agreed to meet up a week later. But he made it clear that at that time he would need a decision. I knew that this time, certainly for me, it would be the biggest one yet!

* * *

The timing was fortuitous, for I had an invitation to a party. One advantage still remaining from my time in Kano, was that I had more or less direct access to several top ICI people, whom I had entertained for days at a time as I showed them round the huge territory for which I was responsible. During those hours spent in hotels, cars and planes we talked of many interesting subjects and swapped personal information in a way that would never have happened across an office desk. Once I even arranged for the deputy chairman of ICI to drive a full-size steam locomotive past our house on the line out of Kano. It was his favourite hobby. I had made it my business to keep in touch, visiting the HQ a couple of times since my return and had been quick to accept an invitation to the annual overseas cocktail party, scheduled for that very week. I was particularly interested in having a chat with George Mason, head of the African department, and only just off the main board, in order to discuss my future. I had come to know him really well on our travels together, and would seriously value his advice.

On arriving at the party I was asked to wear a pin with my name and the word Nigeria on it. These pins were very useful because in that large room there were about 250 people, who worked for the company all over the world. Of course I knew what Mr Mason looked like, badge or no badge, but I couldn't find him anywhere. I did, however, fall into conversation with a very pleasant man of about the same age, who told me that, as far as he knew, Mr Mason was not coming that evening. He and I chatted about West Africa, family, and so on for a while until I saw a friend and excused myself. Before leaving him I said how I had enjoyed our chat, but why wasn't he wearing a badge like everyone else? "Maybe it's because I am the chairman," he said. "Of ICI?" I asked. "Yes," he answered with a smile. Realising I had made another little bloomer, I shook hands and not knowing what else to say, muttered, "Good evening, sir," as I backed away towards my friend.

The following day I phoned Mr Mason's secretary, who rejoiced in the name of Brenda Bracegirdle, asking if she could arrange a short personal meeting. She called me back later asking me to join him at noon for lunch on the Wednesday at the Reform Club, the elite institution not far from head office.

Although the station in Alton was quite near our house, I had never actually used it until the day I needed to catch a train to London's Waterloo for that life-changing (or not) lunch date. I caught a train all right, but from the wrong platform and going in the opposite direction; it had come from Waterloo, and about half an hour before I was due to arrive at the Reform Club to meet Mr Mason, I was alighting at Southampton Central, nearly two hours away from London.

I suppose I could blame my long absences overseas, my poor sense of direction or just plain carelessness. All I knew was that I had committed yet another of those awful mistakes, and could only phone Brenda, who said she would tell Mr Mason that I would be a little late for lunch!

It was more than two hours later that I burst through the revolving doors of the Reform Club, and seeing Mr Mason sitting deep in a brown leather armchair the other side of the huge entrance hall, I blurted out: "I am so sorry…" About ten sets of teeth clashed together with an outpouring of breath to create a mighty "SSHHHHHHH!" I had never been in the Reform Club before, but as I learnt in that moment, it is a very silent place.

Being so late, it was a slightly awkward and hurried affair so I decided to postpone seeking his advice until we adjourned to his office overlooking the Thames. When I explained why I had asked to see him, he made it pretty clear that he was not in a position to offer me anything very exciting in his department for the moment, although it was of course possible that something might come along. How about me? he asked. Did I have any alternatives?

Well, I told him, my sister-in-law did have this boutique. She was starting a mail-order branch and was asking me to run it for her. It would mean moving into London, because of the hours, and the salary would be only £3,000 a year (compared with £4250 for the boring desk job for which I was hoping in HQ).

He stood up and walked to the window, taking in the expansive view over the river, which he must have known so well. He suffered badly from arthritis and I can still see those deformed hands clenching and unclenching behind his back, as he decided my future for me. Finally, he turned and faced me. "Take it, Tony, and good luck to you," he said.

I will never be sure whether he had heard something derogatory about my West African career or, more likely, that he thought there was no hope for a young man who couldn't even catch the right train. Perhaps there simply wasn't a place for me in his department downstairs and he would be glad not to have to create one. But, knowing him as I did, I do believe that he really was giving me his best advice for my own sake. I had explained that I would be running the mail order more or less by myself, and he knew from all our chats in the past that I had always wanted to be my own boss. The next day, having spoken to Fitz, I wrote to thank Mr Mason, following up with my resignation from ICI. Then I cashed in my pension, all this in order to join a boutique in Kensington. B was fine about it, as she prepared to move with the children into Kensington, but CVP was horrified at the thought of my leaving one of Britain's finest established companies so that I could go and work in a b_____ boutique! He never did understand, but I had accepted Fitz's offer and the deed was done. We sold the house for exactly what we had paid for it two years before and the move was made to a mansion flat over the Britannia pub in Allen Street, London, W8. Andrew was to continue at his prep school, while his little sisters joined a nursery school so close that we could see from our sitting room when it was time to pick them up. The pub beneath us was handy, quiet and very convenient when we had guests, as I could nip down to fill one of our huge Victorian jugs with Young's Best Ale!

* * *

Fitz was very fair and agreed to sign a 'service agreement' with me. This was a standard form suggested by CVP and completed by a solicitor friend of ours. It was fairly basic, detailing salary, holidays, terms of employment and an undertaking by both parties that should either ever want to terminate there would be six months' notice or salary in lieu. I kept my copy and Fitz his.

He had a huge amount to do and in spite of the money, which poured daily into the shop, he seemed to have cash-flow problems. However, he found time to teach me how to get the most garments out of a roll of fabric and where to buy and dye buttons, zips and other vital accessories. Most importantly of all, he took me round the East End of London in a van, introducing me to the owners of CMT factories who were to be the bane of my life for nearly two years. CMT stood for cut, make and trim, and that's exactly what these units did. They would agree with me in advance that they would cut and make, for example, 250 satin blouses over sizes 10 to 16, sew on self-covered (with the same fabric) buttons or zips and a Biba label, to be delivered on wire hangers with a polythene cover over each five blouses, within ten days at a price of 17 shillings and sixpence (87.5p) each. Either our driver or I would then drop off the patterns, the right amount of fabric, trimmings and a sample showing the required method and quality, and collect them on the appointed day.

Fitz would tell me which supplier was the most reliable for a given design in quality and delivery, as he had discovered from his own experience in keeping the shop stocked. This was indeed a help for me to get started, but, as I was going to discover, these small factories, many of whom jumped at the extra business I was to offer them, simply couldn't cope. Not only were the quantities for mail order often five or ten times greater than those of the shop, so was the urgency. Shop customers could make another choice or come back next week, but mail order was different. If customers did not receive their specified garments within the promised 28 days, they would be entitled to a refund. The factory owners would come up with every excuse in the book, but this wouldn't help me if I (or sometimes our van driver) turned up to collect three hundred urgently needed garments, to find that only seventy-five were ready!

As the time for the launch approached, Barbara and Fitz worked together on probably the most successful single piece of PR there had ever been in the industry. Their friend Molly Parkin was fashion editor of *The Sunday Times* and they gave her an exclusive, complete with fabulous photographs. I remember Fitz going to Victoria Station at midnight that Saturday to buy ten copies of Sunday's paper, which included a huge double-page spread, entirely devoted to Biba's brand new mail order catalogue.

Corduroy Trench Coat £6-6-0. Skirt £2-10-0.
(Reproduced with the kind permission of the Antiques Collectors Club).

The result was unbelievable. On the Tuesday morning we collected eight bulging sacks from the post office's sorting office, containing nearly 11,000 envelopes. Most of them, as planned, contained requests for the catalogue, and, with the help of the printers, we were able to get these dispatched over the following week or two. The only problem was that many girls had jumped the gun and ordered items chosen from the pictures and prices featured in the paper. This was difficult. We had decided to start with zero stock, so that we could use available fabric and manufacturing capacity for the items that proved to be the most requested when the catalogues themselves reached people. That did make

3
Bonded crepe coat dress. Dressingown collar tied at the side with a bow. Long narrow sleeves with split opening at the wrist. Colours navyor red. Spotted square can be worn at neck.
Price
£4·19·6
For rings, bracelets and scarf see back page.
4
Narrowly cut waistcoat – fully lined. Buttoned and pocketed like the real thing, teams up with front-pleated skirt in honey coloured heavy linen-like rayon.
Price together
£3·19·6
4b
The blouse (can be bought separately) has jugglers' sleeves and rounded collar. The material is black and white spotted silky rayon crêpe
Price
£2·17·6
For rings, bracelets and glasses see back page.

Biba Rayon Waistcoat and Skirt £3-19-6 inc postage and packing (Reproduced with the kind permission of the Antique Collectors' club)

sense, rather than stocking up with items, which, for all we knew, might not be the most popular. But these early orders meant that, from the very beginning, we were behind on manufacture and deliveries. Furthermore, those who ordered without waiting for a catalogue knew nothing of our conditions, especially the one about allowing for 28 days delivery. Of course we could point this out in letters of acknowledgement, which we were now obliged to send out, although they were never part of our plan, but it still meant we were playing catch-up from the outset.

As the thousands of catalogues reached people, including those whose names we had collected from all over the country, the orders came pouring back. The forms clearly said 'Do not send cash' but many of these young girls didn't have bank accounts and couldn't be bothered with postal orders. This meant that, to preserve some kind of security, it was necessary that all orders, some bulging with £10 notes, were opened in full view of my assistant Georgina and me.

I had had a special table made. It was round, covered in white Formica, and seven foot in diameter. In the centre there was a big round hole into which fitted a big black plastic dustbin. Every morning, when our driver arrived from the post office, eight of us would sit around the table, opening the sacks, then the envelopes. Each person's job was to check the money against the items listed, put the order in the relevant pile and throw the cash, PO or cheque into the dustbin! Then we counted it all, ready for banking.

We were usually finished by lunchtime (not that there was ever any time for a break). Individual cards were then written out for each item (an order could contain up to ten items). We put these into specially made pigeonholes on the wall by style, colour and size. While we were all doing this, Fitz would pop in from over the road to see how we had done.

From the beginning, the pigeonholes were necessary, but a nightmare for me. We were always short of cloth and

151

I couldn't place the garment orders without substantial deliveries to our warehouse from the factories. But once the original stock of fabric was exhausted, further deliveries were almost non existent; I couldn't understand why so little came, because the suppliers had given us what we understood were cast-iron repeat guarantees. Our most popular item was a little pinafore dress made from a woven herringbone cloth, which was only available from two suppliers. Neither of them seemed to be able to come up with the fabric we needed, and the piles of cards for that style piled up in its pigeon holes to nearly a thousand over three sizes and two colours. I was exasperated and at a loss as to why this was happening. My hands were tied and I worried night and day, as the complaints grew.

Most evenings, Fitz would appear at the door of our mail-order building making a sign with his hand which meant to join him for a drink in the Catherine Wheel, round the corner. He would buy a couple of large whiskies and I would then have to buy two doubles, which I could ill afford. He would get two more before going. During these hectic sessions, I would find out all sorts of things about how the shop was doing, what publicity was coming up, and any future plans. Of course, what I really wanted was to find out why the cloth suppliers were not keeping to their undertakings. There seemed to be no answer, so when he went off, I would return to work, slightly the worse for wear, with no encouraging news for my long-suffering girls, as they toiled late into the evening.

In the pub, we didn't always talk about Biba; often we touched on our past. Once, when we were talking about National Service, Fitz said he chose not to go for a commission in the army, because being a private soldier was much more fun. He also told me so many funny stories about his life in advertising. He had a great sense of humour and I liked him so much. In spite of all my worries, I looked forward to the little chats we snatched.

There was a time when we got in a fix together. It was during one autumn, when, for no apparent reason, the orders started falling off. Fitz had suspicions about our driver, who seemed to be taking longer and longer in collecting the mail from the main sorting office on Earls Court Road. He had an idea, so early one morning we ordered a mini cab to collect us both and asked the driver to park opposite the sorting office with his engine running. The idea was to follow the driver in the van to see whether he went straight to the office or via his home; it would have been an easy job to drop off half the envelopes for subsequent examination, looking for cash in front of a strong light bulb.

We never did find out. As our cab ticked over that damp and foggy morning, we saw the van go into the sorting office driveway and waited expectantly. Just then all four doors of the minicab opened simultaneously. "POLICE, everybody out!" shouted several voices, and before we knew what, both we and the driver were up against a brick wall being frisked. By the time we were allowed to put our hands down and turn around, the van had gone and we didn't try that again.

Two or three months after the launch of the first catalogue, another beautiful one appeared for the summer. I experienced a real thrill when I opened the first copy. The clothes and the way they were presented with pictures by famous photographers and worn by amazing models, were exquisite. But even as I rejoiced again at being part of such an amazing project, I groaned at the thought of what would happen.

Since many of the original customers were still waiting for their orders, they were upset to receive another catalogue, and many called us up. The lines were jammed, and even if someone did get through, all we could do was to keep them holding on while we checked through the relevant pigeonholes (such as Pinafore Dress, Size 10, Brown). When we found their card, say halfway down the pile, we would try to pacify them by putting it on the top and telling them so. We knew it wouldn't do any good though, because there seemed to be no prospect of receiving enough of the herringbone cloth from which it was to be made, and over the next few days maybe fifty more orders would be put on top of the pile on top of theirs! Sometimes I gave instructions for a refund to be offered, but these girls didn't want their money back. They wanted their DRESS!

After the third or fourth catalogue, Fitz brought in IBM. They sold him machinery, which enabled specially trained operators to produce a punched card for each item ordered. These were in turn put onto a sorting machine, a kind of forerunner of the computer. As a result, each evening I was given long printed lists by style number, size and colour, of all the garments and accessories awaiting dispatch. This did help when answering telephone enquiries, but we still couldn't send many out with so little fabric.

All this time we were operating from what had once been a pretty cottage opposite the back door to the Kensington Church Street shop. Our hard and stressful grind could not have been more different from the colourful, exciting scene we could see through that door. It was fairly dark in the shop, but a quick look would reveal the famous hat stands, hung with every kind of design, fabric and colour. Feather boas lit by coloured spotlights completed the scene, but it was the crowd that really made it. Amidst the booming music there moved a constant stream of customers, all intent on collecting a selection of their favourite styles to try on in the communal changing room in one corner. The occasional boyfriend who had been brought along could be seen lounging on one of the window seats and trying not to look too obvious.

Sometimes, one of the shop girls would run into our office, looking for a size and colour which had run out in the shop, in the hope that she could find one amongst our returns. If she was lucky she would hurry back to the shop and sell it to a grateful customer. She was supposed to bring us the cash, but with crowds blocking the route, this hardly ever happened. Other times a frustrated mail-order customer would fight her way to the till to enquire about her overdue order. She would be told it was nothing to do with the shop, so had to give up. The shop girls knew better than to send them through the back door to us!

Returns were plentiful and a growing problem. The same firm who had designed the catalogue had also produced the box in which orders were to be sent. Shaped like a pillow, it was, like everything else, most beautiful to behold, all in the same black and gold, but it was hardly suitable for its task. Several garments were a tight fit and customers used the same box to send theirs back for a larger size or refund. If it burst open on its way to us, we often didn't know what the contents had been or who had sent them.

At first we tried to handle the returns in our cottage office behind the shop, but Fitz decided that they should be taken separately to our warehouse in Chiswick. There the numbers grew. Still short of production because only a few rolls of cloth arrived from time to time, it was difficult to know where to turn.

Then another catalogue would go out. The clothes were lovely as ever, but people became angry and wrote to the media which recorded the details, often in national newspapers, and the problem escalated. I would work later than ever, trying to catch up with complaints, especially those that came through Esther Rantzen of the *Daily Express* who had taken up the cause of our unfortunate customers. Several times I talked with B about leaving, but we had our rent to pay, the kids' schooling, and so on, and there was no certainty of finding another job, so I had to carry on.

The shop was thronged with customers all day long. It was usually just about empty of stock by the end of the day, but, if a particular cloth ran out, they were able to repeat in small quantities with different fabrics which girls from the design department found in local shops and markets. Of course we couldn't do that because we had to match the photographs in the catalogues and our problems continued. I envied those running the shop because they had no returns either. Their customers came in, tried on, paid and went away happy.

Biba's fame grew and grew on an international basis, and brought famous stars of the sixties into the shop. Twiggy, would pop in. During my time, Marianne Faithful, Mia Farrow, Cilla Black and Yoko Ono all came. On one occasion, word went round that Bridget Bardot was in the shop and I couldn't resist going in, hoping to see my favourite star. Apparently she was quite happy to strip off in the changing room with the rest, but was in fact given a passageway in the back to change on her own. That evening in the pub Fitz confided in me that he stood on a chair in his office and had a peep through the window over the door. I wasn't so lucky!

Most of the time, I missed all this excitement. That was okay. It wasn't my area and I accepted that. But I did take exception whenever either Fitz or Barbara asked me to look after their two Great Danes, Hannibal and Othello, for a few hours. There was no room in our small offices, so they had to be tied up outside. Now and again one of us would have to take them for a walk up the mews, where they were likely to drop a huge turd, usually on the street itself. Sometimes though, in spite of a tug of war, it would land on the smart white doorsteps of one or other of the cottages, inhabited by smart Kensington ladies and gentlemen. When they came shouting outside our door, it presented another problem for me, but I did put my foot down when I was asked to clear up the offending mess.

For the first year, B and I continued renting the flat, but then she inherited some money from her aunt and, with the proceeds of my ICI pension, such as it was, we had the opportunity of raising a sufficient mortgage to buy a small house a couple of miles to the west. The house was at 10 Haarlem Road and cost us £13,000.

This was great. We never had liked spending money on rent, money we would never see again, but it was hard to enjoy the house because it was around that time that I saw even less of the family. As I worked later than ever in the mews, Fitz (after our drink together) started asking me to close the shop before I went home. This meant seeing the staff off at 7pm, cashing up, preparing the bank paying-in slip, turning off all those lights and music, locking everything up, then walking, often with several thousand pounds in cash, to the night safe deposit at the bank. I hated this, especially the moment when my back had to be turned towards all the passers-by, but there was never anyone around to act as a guard as required by our insurance company. To cap it all, soon after I collapsed back at home at about 9pm, Fitz would be on the phone asking how much I had taken!

As the situation deteriorated, I spent my weekends trying to catch up, but it was hopeless. Then, one evening in the

Catherine Wheel, Fitz finally told me that, with the help of a substantial company, they were buying a bigger shop on Kensington High Street, which had once belonged to Daniel Neale, the famous school outfitters, then to Cyril Lord, the carpet people. It was arranged on two large floors with a double-fronted entrance onto the street and a back door for deliveries.

It was the most beautiful shop in London, if not the world! Barbara had worked her magic again and it was amazing to see crowds of girls waiting for opening time in the mornings. Having introduced Fitz to Tim, an old friend of mine, to run this new store, it was decided that I was to give him a hand by running the production side for both the shop and the mail order, if and when any cloth arrived. Customer demand in the new shop was insatiable and it was not at all unusual to see a battle going on between two girls who wanted the same dress. Deliveries came in through the door at the back that opened onto a smaller street, but our fans found this out and, especially when the famous coloured canvas boots arrived, our drivers were in real danger as they were mobbed all their way to the stock room.

I remember one particular time when the shop offered rubberised raincoats. They were an excellent design of course, a lovely shape with wide lapels and belt at a very reasonable price. So popular were they that they ran out most days. I had a similar one which I had bought in Austin Reed two years earlier, and one morning on Tim's day off, having fought my way through the rain and the mob to get into the shop half an hour before we opened up, I hung it briefly on a hat stand. I prepared all the tills for the day, then opened up to admit the crowd. Clean forgetting my coat, I then returned to my office.

It got sold and I never saw it again. That was Biba. Wonderful. Crazy. Thrilling. Unforgettable Biba!

* * *

There was a further business development. It transpired that the company that had invested in the project was itself bought out by an even greater, public company. This opened up a bigger future for Biba as history will show, but it wasn't good for me.

The new people didn't like mail order, and I was told that, once the sixth catalogue was finished, there would be no more. Even this proved difficult, because, although the much-needed money poured in as usual, only about half the orders could be satisfied. Furthermore, I had an endless number of claims and complaints from previous catalogues to answer. Eventually, as the new investors became more involved, it was decided that they would provide the money to refund all undelivered orders and returns. At first this proved to be good news, and my staff wrote cheques for the requisite amount, pinning them to the relevant documentation, before they were passed to me for signature. There were over two thousand altogether, but we got them done and dispatched. Gradually the phones stopped ringing, then my faithful staff lost their jobs, and the mail order closed down. To this day, at the very mention of Biba, I meet women of a certain age who never got their pinafore dress! I was both relieved and broken hearted, but even as we closed the warehouse and office, I knew I had done my best and still had a job.

As the new company started to move in, there came experienced retail people in grey suits who worked only with figures. More and more I found myself involved in the store (not 'shop' any more) doing stock checks, evaluations, early opening and late closing, production and, very occasionally, PR. This last intrigued me, having witnessed the huge amount of free publicity that had been the basis of Biba's early success. There was a small but very efficient PR department in the office building, but they couldn't be everywhere, and sometimes I found myself looking after fashion writers who walked into the shop, looking for a story and hoping to borrow samples for photography. It was important not to interfere with the successful efforts of the PR department and to ask if they could send someone down, but it was often in the evening when their office had closed and they had gone home. In this way I was instrumental in achieving a small amount of extra coverage and in the process made some good friends, some of them quite influential fashion writers. The next day, I was always careful to tell the PR people what had transpired, so they could follow it up.

One day Fitz sent for me at lunchtime. Sitting with a cigarette on his faux zebra skin sofa, he came straight to the point, saying that the new firm, which had paid all those mail-order cheques, was only prepared to proceed with further investment in Biba, if the latter was completely unfettered. In looking through Fitz's personnel file, they had come across his copy of my six months' service agreement, by this time over two years old, and had raised a query.

Fitz went on to say that Biba had a great future potentially with a huge injection of money. He even mentioned the possibility of buying a massive department store on Kensington High Street with the help of these people and was anxious that their negotiations would continue without hindrance. Accordingly, he asked, was I prepared to discontinue our legal agreement?

I responded that I would never deliberately stand in the way of family success and that I was really excited about the expansion of the wonderful things he and Barbara had so far achieved. Fitz said they both appreciated my expressing this, adding that it would be of enormous help to that very expansion if we could jointly destroy both copies of the agreement. I promised to bring mine in the next morning.

All this time, I worshipped Barbara for everything she had created, and constantly sang her praises. I believe she knew what I was going through, and was really nice to me. Several times, she invited B and me to dinner in their lovely house. It was always fun, and I remember laughing at the huge amount of loaves which were stacked on the shelves in her kitchen. I believe it was because Fitz was trying to lose weight, but still bought the bread to see how much he was not eating!

I became really fond of Fitz as well, although, with everything that was going on, I would hesitate to say we were friends. We had some good times together in the pub. He often said he appreciated how I had fought to overcome the impossible problems caused by the failure of some of our fabric suppliers, to give us the promised backing. After we had destroyed the agreements, he said I would be transferred to the new store, but I knew this would be difficult because I had only recently introduced Tim to do the job.

So it proved. Although I opened the store some mornings and helped with the production, it was quite apparent that I was becoming redundant. I worried about where this situation was leading, and one morning I saw Fitz in his office to ask him. After a few minutes, our conversation became heated, and it was decided that I should leave immediately with a cheque in my pocket for a month's salary.

I shook Fitz by the hand, and walked sadly down to the store where I had left my coat on opening up that morning. Fitz had evidently called down, because Tim was standing there with my coat, saying that he would rather I didn't come in! We do laugh about it these days, but it sure was awkward at the time.

As the number 73 bus trundled westwards along Kensington High Street towards home, I sat upstairs, it has to be said, in a bit of a state. I do confess there were tears in my eyes. For all the frustration and long hours, I had been thrilled to be involved and was looking forward to becoming part of 'Big Biba'. Now this. What on earth was I to do? What a shock it would be when I got home and told B. There seemed to be no answer, I was thirty-five and in trouble. So was B and our young family. Our house too, was in danger of being lost. My salary had not changed in two years and we had very little in the bank.

All of a sudden, something in my head told me, *Do something!* I stood up, got off the bus, crossed the road and caught one going the other way into London's West End. Walking quickly to 15 Savile Row, I climbed to the fifth floor (there was no lift) and knocked on the door of my friend Ken Riley, who operated a successful commercial design business from there.

Before the end of the day, I had hired a desk and chair in the corner of his large open room for £15 a week, and applied for a telephone. Ken created for me a smart sign that said, 'Tony Porter & Associates, Public Relations Consultants, 5th Floor', which I stuck neatly on the wall in the downstairs hallway. I didn't have any 'Associates', but it sounded good! By the time I got home that evening, I was able to tell B that I had started a new business. So much better than giving her a shock by saying I no longer worked for her sister, and what on earth were we going to do?

A few months later, Biba Ltd bought Kensington's Derry and Toms, a massive department store of original art deco design, built in the 1930s. The rest is history.

As for me, as I walked through Hyde Park the next morning on the way to my Savile Row office, I swore that henceforth I would never be employed by anyone else. I would work only for my family and ME! Little did I know how true this oath would become in the years to come.

CHAPTER EIGHT

I t took no time to get a telephone number and to print the business cards Ken had designed for me. They were in brown and cream, with stitch-like markings reminiscent of a clothing label, a bit naff really, but they worked okay, as time went by.

The main idea of public relations is to obtain editorial coverage in the media for a given company or its products; in the case of the fashion industry, of course, this very much means pictures as well as words. Such publicity, unlike expensive advertising, is free and infinitely more persuasive; if the fashion editor of your favourite magazine or newspaper writes that the dress or jacket pictured above is what you should be wearing for the forthcoming season, it means so much more than an advertisement, obviously paid for by the manufacturers themselves, blowing their own trumpet. Furthermore, not only the space but all attendant costs, such as the photographer, studio and model, are also free, paid for by the publication.

I set off round the rag trade district on day one, cold calling, as I described the joys and benefits of PR. Naturally I chose fashion houses who, I could tell from a glance in their windows, offered merchandise which would be of most interest to the press. Having asked to see the sales manager, I would explain to him or her how, in exchange for a small monthly retainer, I could get their company's products featured in the *Daily Telegraph*, *Woman's Own* or even *Vogue*. Of course my pitch wasn't successful every time. Although it was quite an easy message to get across, people were not always persuaded. I carried magazines and newspapers in my briefcase to illustrate my point, but, starting from scratch as I was, I couldn't claim that a single one had been as a result of my own work. Perhaps understandably, this proved to be a problem! Nevertheless, I did get interest here and there, often from houses that saw their competitors' garments in my sample publications, and thought how good it would be if theirs started appearing in the same way.

The tricky bit came when I was asked how much I would charge. Some wanted to pay by the square inch, with a sliding scale according to the importance to them of each publication. Far too complicated, I would say, and bring them back, if I could, to my original suggestion of a retainer. After a fair amount of argy-bargy, I would eventually settle on anything from £250 per month for a large dress or coat house down to £50 per month for accessories like hats, jewellery or shoes. These fees were to grow rapidly as good results started appearing, but for the time being, only two weeks after the birth of my little business, I was happy to have five accounts worth nearly £6,000 per annum, twice what I had earned at Biba for the last couple of years, and weekends off too! My only expenses were £15 a week for the desk and any phone bills, plus my return bus fare from home to Notting Hill Gate and back. I walked the other couple of miles through Kensington Gardens and Hyde Park to get fresh air and exercise. Later, as my business grew, other expenses came along, such as wages and entertainment, but at the outset there was absolutely no question of incurring any of these, for the perfectly good reason that I didn't yet have the money!

As I strode through the park every morning, it was with a singing heart. At last I was my own boss and I could organise every hour of every day. All through my school days, the army, Africa, ICI and Biba, there had always been someone, near or far, to tell me what to do and when to do it. All these situations had come to an end through matters beyond my control. Now at last it was all up to me. Any ideas or extra effort I put in were for my own benefit and of course, that of my family. There was a risk, because I could never again count on that vital cheque on the last day of each month, but I promised myself that, if it all went wrong, I would not complain. The decision to strike out on my own, instead of seeking another job, was mine and mine alone. I learnt to look only forward, never back. Years later, I was to read a quote by Anna Wintour, the celebrated editor of *American Vogue*, in which she said that having to leave a job is good for you. Well, it certainly wasn't like that at the time, but after the first few months it was already beginning to feel that way for me.

I was a most unusual fashion PR consultant. Most of those operating at that time were good-looking girls who dressed in their clients' merchandise, and took journalists, often also attractive, out to coffee or lunch to discuss some fashion statement or perhaps a photographic shoot. I was not a girl, nor was I particularly attractive and, at the age of thirty-five, must have looked totally out of place, walking into, say, *Petticoat* magazine's fashion office, with dresses over my arm and a bag full of shoes, hats and plastic jewellery to match!

I suppose I never got over this, though I found that I was a little less obvious when I stopped wearing a suit and tie. While never approaching trendiness, I did look a bit more casual amongst all that high fashion! Back in the office, I worked incessantly on the phone, ringing the fashion editorial offices of all the important publications to establish what they needed for their next feature and whether I could help with relevant garments or accessories. Often I got the brush off from journalists or their secretaries who were far too busy to talk to me. However, now and again I hit the jackpot, when some fashion assistant would ask for a whole outfit to be brought to a studio for a photographic shoot, sometimes that very afternoon. This could result, two to three months later, in a whole colour page in, say, *Cosmopolitan*, or part of a feature in major newspapers like the *Daily Telegraph* or *Daily Mirror*, much sooner, because of their shorter copy dates. Often pictures would feature items from several of my clients, all of whom would be delighted at seeing their products and their name in the paper, complete with the price of the item, and where it could be bought. Before long, as the value of PR struck home, I was able to start raising my fees, more closely to match the results I was getting.

Within six months, I felt I should move premises. By then I had befriended a growing group of journalists, who liked the idea of popping in to see if I had anything suitable for their next feature. But there were a couple of snags. Although the building in Savile Row was easy to find, in that it housed the main showroom of Hardy Amies, one of the Queen's favourite couturiers, not many busy writers had time to 'pop' up five floors! Furthermore, even if one or more of them had climbed up to my office, it would have been difficult to show them a range of clothing in the corner of Ken's big room, full of people playing Radio Caroline as they designed labels and book covers.

I did a deal with Outlander, my knitwear account, whereby half my fee would take the form of exclusive use of the first floor of their building just off Regent Street. Their cleverly styled outfits were amazing, and much sought after by the fashion editors of newspapers and magazines who loved to call in to my 'showroom' to see the latest arrivals. While the kettle was boiling and I had them in my grasp, so to speak, I showed them other things as well, and it worked a treat. They would often go off with a selection of sweaters, complemented by shoes, hats and other accessories (all from my clients, of course), which they needed for a really substantial feature. Sometimes I would send them to their office or direct to the studio. I was especially well placed for *Vogue*, whose back door was just opposite our building on Maddox Street. Sometimes I would bump into girls ('Voguettes' as they were called) from their fashion department, and ask them in to see our ranges. Time and again I was able to lend them exactly what they needed, and months later there would be a beautiful sweater or hat featured in *Vogue*.

Outlander was owned by Jose, a big fun Cuban, who liked to stand outside on a summer's day, smoking a fat cigar and watching the girls go by, and Costas, a smooth Greek, connected to a shipping line, who came to work every day in one of the big new Range Rovers. It was typical of him to have had the letters 'RANGE ROVER' on the front of the bonnet changed so that they read 'HANG OVER'! They became really good friends of ours and over the years we were well rewarded for the enormous amount of coverage we achieved for them and their popular products.

The problem of my newfound success was that I was completely tied to my showroom in case of an unexpected visitor, and I began to look for an assistant to help me out. Pretty soon I found Joy, who was working in the PR section of Courtaulds. She was looking for a move and when my interview with her went well, I offered her the job. She said she would let me know, but when two weeks went by without an answer, I got impatient, wondering why there was such a delay. Then I found out. Her father, who was a director of Marks and Spencer, had initiated questions about me around the industry before he encouraged her to take the job. Several people in the trade had told me they had received enquiries and I must have passed the examination, because, soon afterwards, Joy rang to accept the position.

Now I didn't have to slog backwards and forwards to Fleet Street, and, as first Joy and, in due course, other assistants, handled the press so well, I was able to take on more clients. There was a limit, though, as there could be a danger of one client's products clashing with another's. I had time to cast my net wider, so when a young American in our street asked me at the bar in the Mason's Arms one day whether I could publicise his newly imported waterbeds, I didn't say no!

People were beginning to talk about them as a really comfortable sleep, because, once you settled and remained still, the water in the mattress assumed your shape and supported you at all points equally. This meant there were no pressure points, so you never had to turn over in your sleep. Anyway, this was the message my new client Ed asked me to put out in return for a generous fee.

I quickly found that, in spite of all these expansive claims, they were still not selling very well because potential customers feared they would burst. Ed assured me that the beds were really strongly sealed against leakage, and that this could not happen. Accordingly, I hatched a plan, whereby I approached Chessington Zoo. Asking if we could take a photograph of an elephant lying comfortably on a waterbed, I planned to mail it to national and regional newspapers, with resultant publicity for the zoo and for my new client.

I made the arrangements, engaging a photographer, transport, and so on. All concerned approved this brilliant idea of mine, but not for long. As the giant animal was led onto the full double-size waterbed, all seemed well, until his keeper urged him to lie down. Alas! A giant wave of cold water gushed in all directions, soaking everyone, including my photographer and all his equipment!

Not such a good idea then. Fortunately, there were no other cameramen around who might have taken pictures that would have been easily sold to the press for all the wrong reasons! Neither Ed nor I would have been glad to see one of those the next morning in our favourite newspaper. We did subsequently retake the picture, using a perfectly dry baby elephant, but somehow the prints that I mailed out didn't bear such a reassuring message, and Ed wasn't so pleased with the results. Maybe, I thought, I'd better stick to fashion!

On another occasion, a journalist from the *Daily Telegraph*, having visited several clients with Joy, advised us that she planned to feature a raincoat from our client Four Seasons and a sweater from Outlander, and we gave her full details for the relevant credits, including stockists and prices. We proudly told our respective clients to buy the paper the next day. They did too, but neither of them picked up the phone to congratulate us on the two large and beautiful pictures. The detailed credits had been printed the wrong way round! Both clients got calls all right, all day, but found them very irritating. Four Seasons didn't make sweaters and Outlander didn't make raincoats. You win some…!

* * *

Overall though, things were going better than ever. There were wages to pay and new expenses like taxis and lunches; I had even appointed an accountant who advised me and did my tax return. All this cost money, but with an increasing number of contented clients, my income had gone up again. One evening in 1974, B and I sat down, did our sums, and decided that at long last, we could afford a holiday, so why not!

That first time we took the children to Brittany, renting a small house (for some reason called Flocon de Neige [snowflake]) with friends. We toured all the ancient sites when it rained, and enjoyed the sandy beach when the sun came out. It was a happy time with many laughs, not least when one little boy, as his dad returned from a swim, greeted him pointing down at his bucket full of water saying: "Look, Daddy, I've washed your camera for you!"

Then I fell in love with a car. It was one of those Citroëns (ID 19) that went up and down by a clever use of hydraulics and even the headlights turned when you went round a corner. This one was unusual, because it was a convertible. We painted it a trendy milk chocolate brown. The children loved it, especially when we took it on holiday with another family to France, where it was much admired.

Our favourite car EVER

We made the best of it in the sunshine, and one day drove the car, piled high with people, down a sandy track which led from our rented house along the top of the beach and found a little café with a ping-pong table. We stayed there most of the day enjoying the beach and retiring to the cafe for wine, ping pong, lunch, more ping pong and more wine. About 5pm, the café owner announced that we were in such a state that he could not legally sell us any more wine, but that he was allowed to give it to us instead! By the time we set off very slowly in our open Citroën, back along that sandy track to our house, I am ashamed to say we adults were in a bit of a state. Gwenda, one of the young mums, didn't shut her door properly. When it opened and she fell out, laughing helplessly as she lay in the sand. It just added to the fun!

We kept that beautiful car for another year, but underneath the rust was working away and it started sagging in the middle; a little later, the doors wouldn't stay shut, so we had to part-exchange it (valued at £90!) for a newer, smaller car, which had reliability, but none of the beauty of our *décapotable*. Twenty years later, with the help of the *Citroënean* magazine, I discovered that an Australian couple, on holiday here, had come across it (painted white with emulsion paint!). Having bought it more or less as scrap, they put it on a ship to Sydney. On the way, apparently it broke in two, presumably because of that rusty chassis. By the time I discovered the car (818 FYT), it was nearing completion not far from Cairns, and the owners were kind enough to send me a photograph. These cars are extremely rare, and as I write, I can report that only yesterday I saw one featured on TV, fully restored and for sale at £150,000!

Later, we had other holidays when we flew down to Tunisia and Ampurias in northern Spain, which became a family favourite, even though we were plagued by rats scampering around above our heads in the attic of the villa! When the owner refused to help, we made up a sort of extension lead with a 100-watt bulb on the end and led it up into the roof space. The rats certainly didn't like that. Either they moved out or tiptoed around from then onwards.

Back in England, my friend Bruce took B and me for a sail down the river Hamble near Southampton. He had the most beautiful old classic two-masted ketch called *Thalia*. We quickly became hooked on the graceful movement and sound as she cut through the waters around the Isle of Wight. Before long we were on the hunt, and found ourselves a second-hand sloop (only one mast) called a Westerly Longbow. Bruce came aboard to give me a lesson, and we had some hairy moments on the river, perhaps the worst concerning the tiller. This, as most people know, is connected to the rudder, which, being specially shaped and positioned underneath the water, is designed to direct which way the boat goes.

So that the tiller can be removed and stowed when the boat is not in use, it is held in place by a strong bolt with a big chrome nut on the end, and it is vital that this nut is kept really tight when sailing. Well, nobody had told me this at the time and, having coaxed the yacht up to five knots, heading straight down river with a following wind, I suddenly found myself with the tiller in my hand not connected to anything! Bruce, who was up in the bow, shouted to me to help him get the sails down to slow the boat before I collided with one of the three boats heading up river towards me. Even then, it was still impossible to reassemble the thing properly while the boat was moving but she eventually came to a halt by gently ramming a wooden pontoon. A small amount of damage was done to the boat and to the pontoon, but I got away with it and had learnt my lesson.

I didn't take her out again until I had undertaken professional training and passed my onshore skipper's exam. After that, B and I both took further courses, including navigation and boat handling, enabling us to cruise far and wide. First we went to France and the Channel Islands, then to the Scilly Isles off the southwesterly tip of Cornwall. They were idyllic, but almost completely surrounded by jagged rocks, often just below the surface. We would post one of the children up in the bow, who would shout "Daddy, there's a rock over there!" then "Go left [should be 'hard a' port']. There's a big black one just under the water!"

Much later, we chartered boats in the Caribbean, Thailand and Croatia. With all this experience, I became a member of the Royal Thames Yacht Club. Having been proposed and seconded, the wait to join had been very long, but I now proudly flew the blue ensign when I was aboard, and became very active during the racing season. It was not as a participant, but as a marshal, bouncing up and down far out to sea, a gin and tonic in hand, counting the fleet round the marks, and giving a full report about whose right of way it was if one boat hit another on my patch!

Sitting as it was, opposite Harvey Nichols in Knightsbridge, London, miles from the sea, the RTYC club house was pretty useless when we were on a sailing weekend, but good for meetings, administration and entertainment. This seemed good for me, and it was with some pride that I invited Ann Chubb, another fashion writer on the *Daily Telegraph*, to join me there for lunch. Very different, I thought, from the normal run of restaurants to which she was invited by my fellow PRs. I got there in good time and sat in the upstairs bar with a drink, reading that day's carefully selected *Daily Telegraph*.

Five minutes after the appointed time, I heard voices from the hallway downstairs. I took no notice at first but the voices became louder and angrier. As I listened, I realised two things: firstly that one of the voices belonged to my important guest, and secondly that the other one, belonging to the uniformed hall porter, was telling her to use the side entrance. When she asked why, I heard him reply that it was because she was a woman! Hurrying down, I did my best to sort things out, explaining that I was a new member, and an exception was made, but embarrassment persisted, and lunch that day was not a success. Thenceforth I entertained my guests in well-known West End restaurants!

We were particularly fond of Lesley Ebbetts, another journalist, who lived near us. She was fashion editor of the *Daily Mirror* and always great fun. She spent the weekend on the yacht with us soon after the end of the Falklands War, and we were all excited to see a huge ship steaming down the Solent towards us. She passed so close to us that we could clearly see the name *Canberra* on her bow, and hundreds of men waving at us. A few of them were cheering too, but the whole lot joined in when Lesley, who was waving frantically with both arms over her head, suddenly lost her boob tube, the fashionable top of the time! She was always up to date with what she wore, and afterwards told us how, turning up at a London club in a slinky trouser suit, she was told by the doorman that trousers for ladies were not permitted. Okay, she said, took them off, put them in her bag, and entered wearing the perfectly decent top half!

I suppose I should be able to describe myself as a competent skipper, but our logbooks, which describe many a long voyage in detail, do include some really hairy situations. However, helped by B's growing skills at the chart table and all around the boat, I usually managed to execute the right manoeuvre, sometimes only just in time, in any given predicament! Slowly, the children too came to put their faith in me and they performed as useful members of the crew. We all used to laugh when Julia, working hard with two hands on one of the chrome winches would chant:

> "I must, I must, I must develop my bust.
> The bigger the better, the tighter the sweater,
> The boys are depending on us."
> And later:"I will, I will, I will improve it still."
> And later still:"Hurrah, hurrah, I need a bigger bra!"

Many friends of ours and of the children joined us and, quite apart from the actual sailing, we had enormous fun. Our favourite, Mary, who, after working for us for several years, left to become a director of Russell and Bromley shoes, came for a weekend aboard, wearing, much to my disgust, a brand-new pair of expensive high-heeled shoes. Thinking of the potential damage to my deck, I persuaded her to remove them, which she duly did, putting them down carefully by the mast. Somehow or other, a rope must have entwined itself round one of the shoes which then fell over the side while we were tied up at Buckler's Hard on the Beaulieu River. When she stopped crying (Mary cried a lot!), I said, "Well, you won't be needing this one will you?" and wickedly dropped the other offending shoe into the fast flowing river. Later the first one was found caught up in weed on the surface, but not the second. I was in awful trouble, but for future voyages she always wore soft, flat shoes, a bit kinder to my deck!

There was another time when we set sail with a brand-new spinnaker (a 'balloon' sail used when the wind is coming from behind – or should I say 'aft'). B had created a striking design in four different colours, which we had made up and we were really proud when we raised it for the first time on the Saturday morning. The Solent waters were crowded with yachts of all sizes as we gathered speed before a brisk easterly.

As long as you are under sail (no engine) and in open water, there is no speed limit, but I must say I began to wonder whether I was breaking some law when a huge and very noisy khaki-coloured helicopter appeared above us. It seemed to pick us out, as it hovered menacingly, apparently only a few feet above our new sail and I thought hard about what other sin I could be committing. In order to look innocent and friendly, we all waved, although we couldn't see any of the crew from that angle, and the machine eventually climbed away from us, disappearing into the distance.

Not knowing what to think but fearing some kind of 'ticket', I forgot about it until, a week later, we received through the post a colourful set of photographs, depicting our fine new spinnaker full of wind. That was when Julia admitted that she had arranged the whole thing with a boyfriend who flew helicopters for the army!

[Nice one Julia]

Over the years we bought bigger and better boats and used them nearly every weekend from Easter to November. Later, when we were finally to sell our lovely Moody 34 and leave, the harbour master at the marina told us he had never seen a boat so regularly used. Many expensive yachts sat on their berths week after week, while their owners ate and drank. One, on a pontoon near us, even had window boxes with bright red geraniums! The only person who didn't like our boat so much was CVP, who used to look forward so much to our spending the weekend with them in Sussex. Of course, we couldn't always make it, though. Once, when I called to say that we couldn't visit them because we were sailing with friends that weekend, I heard him mutter, as he put down the phone, "Bloody boat." I'm afraid he meant it. Later, to make amends, we arranged to sail into Chichester, where he and Phyl were staying in a small harbourside hotel. The idea was that they would at last come aboard for a Jim Porter, but even that turned into an unfortunate occasion. At the age of eighty, he couldn't swing his damaged leg over the guardrail to get on board. To this very day it makes me so sad to write about that moment.

As I have said, I started my little business alone. Then there was Joy and then Maria, a beautiful Greek girl who had worked for Pringle and had many good press contacts. For nearly a year we thrived as a team and our client list grew, but then Joy left to start her own business and Maria moved away from London. This meant that, quite suddenly, I had to find and train two new girls in a short time. I found them all right, but just then I fell ill.

I mentioned earlier that one of our holidays was in Tunisia. The villa there had a swimming pool, which we used a lot, but its water wasn't properly treated and I contracted an ear infection. It was very stubborn and, as I was told later, it managed to penetrate firstly my inner ear, then my central nervous system. The result, after a month or so, was manic depression, which reached its peak at a time when I was still attempting to show these two girls how we operated, and to introduce them to our fourteen clients.

It is hard to explain after all this time how I felt. Suffice to say that I didn't want to get up in the morning, or make myself smart or walk through the park. Similarly, I had no will to encourage these new assistants, and no way of resisting a short temper from which I had never suffered before.

It was the most unfortunate timing and the two new girls took full advantage of the situation. They seldom turned up on time or paid much attention to this new boss who wandered in late, dressed in jeans and an old sweater. Gradually the phone calls from my long-nurtured fashion writers, who had regularly featured the products of our clients, dried up. Simultaneously, those very clients started calling to ask why they were not getting publicity any more. My business was in free fall, and in spite of a course of medication prescribed by my doctor, I seemed to be getting no better. There was apparently nothing I could do about it.

But B could. She issued each of the children (Caroline, the youngest, was nine by then) with a key to access the house after school and told them we would be home by six. She then accompanied me to the office every day and took over. The first thing she did was to sack those two lazy girls, and then found a bright junior whom she trained in the art of PR (she was only just learning herself!). Quickly, she stopped the rot and when my pills finally began to work, the phones were ringing again – for all the right reasons. It took six months, but one day the doctor signed me off and I took over my own business again. Of course I wasn't going to let B go though and we made a great team from then on, even if it did mean lugging the family shopping to the car park before we drove home through the traffic. The days of walking through the park were over for me!

CHAPTER NINE

Not only had B saved us, but by staying with me as she did, she enabled me to branch out into other sections of fashion promotion. The first of these was to result in the foundation of British Fashion Week.

For a long time there had always been the Prêt à Porter week in Paris twice a year, then in Milan there sprung up the Milano Vende Moda, followed by similar shows in the USA, Germany and Japan. In London, there had been small groups who had got together in Chelsea Town Hall and elsewhere, then Britain had hit the headlines with Mary Quant's mini skirt and Biba in the Swinging Sixties. But there had been no lasting joint or corporate effort to establish an event carefully timed to be covered by the world's busy press and buyers in a few days. Now, here we were, towards the end of 1974, with a multitude of talent pouring out of colleges like St Martin's School of Art and the London College of Fashion, all wanting to show their new work, but with no international event through which to do it. Similarly, our established designers, while making stalwart individual efforts, were not part of an organised event.

There existed a quasi-government body called the Clothing Export Council of Great Britain, whose job it was to promote the sale of British clothing overseas and in the autumn of 1974, it was to its director Peter Randle that I went. Wasn't it about time, I asked him, that we should form some sort of association and agree a date in the calendar, when all its selected designers would show their collections for the forthcoming season? Then it would be possible for overseas buyers and press to ensure that, during that period, usually the inside of a week not clashing with Paris or Milan, they would definitely be in London for the British shows, including student presentations.

After several meetings in Mr Randle's office, attended by myself and some of the top people in the industry, he said he would give the idea his backing, and asked me to formulate a programme. He also agreed that, if I could persuade five top designers to contribute £100 each, he would match it, thus making £1,000 available for the printing and mailing of our very first brochure, entitled 'British Fashion Week'.

Dates were agreed, and I made appointments in order to discuss with our top designers which venue and time they would choose, so that visitors could easily attend each show without wasting time or having to double back through the London traffic. Some of the top five designers who agreed all those years ago have closed now, or sadly died, but I want to record their names as Jean Muir, Zandra Rhodes, Bill Gibb, Bruce Oldfield and John Bates.

Jean Muir's sketch for Autumn British Fashion Week 1975
(Reproduced from an original sketch,
donated to the author in 1975)

They each came up with beautiful sketches and their hundred pounds and, with the promised extra five hundred, I set about the design and printing of a brochure. I could not have done it without them.

As we spread the word, other great designers, including Caroline Charles and Betty Jackson, joined in with their own individual shows. Also to be included were the London Designer Collections headed by Annette Worsley Taylor, who, in years to come, was to earn an MBE for all the work she did in heading up London Fashion Week, (as it came to be called) and The New Wave, with Lesley Goring. Thus my first brochure included a mass of young fashion excitement and no fashion journalist or buyer, who was worth his or her salt, could risk being elsewhere that week.

First, I mailed important press in Britain, Europe, America and Asia, enclosing the brochure and an invitation which gave my own contact numbers for any special requests. After that I still had some of my thousand pounds, and determined to use this to help provide a very special service to the top doyens of the world's fashion press. I helped them to book (but not pay!) their London hotels and met them in a chauffeured car when they arrived at Heathrow or Gatwick Airport. During the journey to their hotels, I would furnish them with full information about the week's special events and any rising stars. I even prevailed upon the Clothing Export Council to pay for another big car in which I ferried the top international three, Bernadine Morris (*New York Times*) Hebe d'Orsay (*International Herald Tribune*) and Marylou Luther (*Los Angeles Times*) from show to show. We became very close to these three ladies, and, on one occasion, Hebe asked B to take her shopping down the King's Road! Years later, when we were in Los Angeles, Marylou and her husband invited us to stay, showing us the art deco sights and even lent us their great big Lincoln Continental to drive around town. I didn't have my licence with me, but B did and did a great job in all that traffic!

It worked a treat. Every top journalist I had invited had made it their business, through their columns, to alert the main buyers back in their own countries. So the attendance, especially for such a new event, was outstanding, with substantial orders making it all worthwhile. My active part in all this was appreciated by most, but not all, PRs of partaking designers, who had reserved front-row seats for when I arrived at their shows, introducing a 'Royal Flush' of international journalists! Glowing reports (if the designs were good enough, of course) would appear in major international newspapers, sometimes the very next day, as a result of long international calls made from hotel bedrooms (no emails or mobiles then!).

This was just the beginning. In due course we were joined by Percy Savage with his substantial Fashion Promotions group at the Inn on the Park and then the huge trade exhibition at Olympia led by Caroline de Courcy Ireland. As the number of participants and visitors grew, just as they had in other long-established world venues, so did the publicity. As a result, these days it is difficult to avoid the vast TV and press coverage, twice a year, of London Fashion Week, with its associated hype and massive exhibitions. For me, it meant nothing in terms of direct financial reward, because the Clothing Export Council still had no budget for this purpose. But it did mean that, over the years, I sat on many committees, getting to know everyone who was important in the industry. In addition, of course, I was able to keep an eye open for those companies who were looking for a good PR, and more than once I admit having fed a promising name to my excellent team back in the showroom of Tony Porter and Associates. They did the rest!

I cannot say that PR always served me well. Any publicity is supposed to be good publicity, but there was one occasion when this was, to say the least, doubtful. Through Fashion Week, I had come to know the Fashion Editor of *The Times*, Prudence Glyn, and she once rang me, asking if I was free the following day. It seemed that she wanted to feature a double-breasted suit by Saint Laurent in her paper, and enquired whether I would model it for her. Always anxious to please, and believing that an appearance in *The Times*, with a credit naming me as a fashion consultant, couldn't be a bad thing, so I agreed to meet her at the studio in the morning.

The shoot went well, and Pru, in thanking me, told me to look in the paper on the following Monday, when she expected it to appear. It appeared all right, quite a small, black-and-white picture of me in a fairly boring grey suit. Underneath, she had written a caption, describing the garment and giving the name of the stockist in Bond Street where her readers could buy it. So far so good, but then she added: "It is modelled here by Tony Porter, public relations consultant, in the West End of London. He told me that he couldn't afford the suit at £299, but you should have seen the yearning in his eyes!" Oh NO!

Undaunted, I even started my own model agency. One day, as I walked around the exhibition at Olympia, I couldn't help noticing a tall girl who was modelling on one of the lesser-known stands. Quite apart from her height, she was striking, to say the least. Of course, it would have been unethical for me to approach her there on her stand, but when I saw her later in the tea queue, I engaged her in conversation in order to ascertain whether or not she had an agent. In a pronounced northern accent, she said she didn't and that she was just helping a friend. I advised her to get one and gave her my brown visiting card to enable her to contact me for further advice.

Her name was Sally Gilbertson and she came to see me in Maddox Street when Fashion Week was over. After asking B and the girls what they thought, I told Sally that we could launch her as a professional model, and she jumped at the chance. The following Friday, following a short press release from me, there was a headline in the *Draper's Record*, the leading trade magazine, announcing "Tony Porter Launches Model Agency"!

We did well for her too. Christopher Moore, even then one of the best-known fashion photographers, helped to create a really good portfolio and our own PR girls made appointments for Sally with the fashion editors of the best young magazines.

She was featured in many a piece over the ensuing six months and even appeared on front covers three times (including *Miss London* and *Girl About Town* which were leading free publications at the time). She made her name and good money too. The trouble was that she was our only model, so, when we were asked for 'Z cards' showing the other models on our books, we had to say that there weren't any! No more girls approached us, and in due course, Sally herself started meeting other models who were represented by big agencies like Models One with branches in the fashion capitals of the world.

Perhaps inevitably, she came to me one day to say that she was going elsewhere. Grateful as she was, she felt that it would be better for her. She was right too. After nearly a year of success in London, she moved to Japan, where her particular height and look were in great demand. We lost touch, but last I heard she was heading towards supermodel status there. That was nearly twenty-five years ago, so for all I know she might be a granny by now!

* * *

Another name I picked up was that of India Imports, founded and fully owned by Mr Lakhi Paintal. I first met him on his stand at a fashion week exhibition, and marvelled at the most beautiful, inexpensive Indian clothes he was offering. They were all in the softest cotton which had been hand printed, using intricately carved wooden blocks, in Rajasthan, then made up into dresses and separates by small factories in and around New Delhi.

His story and products were crying out for publicity and he invited us to his home to discuss what we could do for him. This was the start of a long friendship between our two families and of commercial success for us all. When B and her (by then) two assistants showed the collection to the fashion editors, they positively pounced on it and for weeks on end, selected samples were taken to studios for photography. They were so photogenic that they always appeared in the largest pictures and we had whole pages in *Cosmopolitan, Woman's Own, Country Life, Daily Mail.* Jean Scroggie, the much loved and respected *Daily Telegraph* fashion and travel writer, featured them over and over again. Lakhi could not believe how famous, popular and successful we had made his company in three short months and invited us both to India, not only to celebrate, but for B to advise him on his next collection.

Altogether we were to fly to that fascinating and mysterious country seven times, and, as Lakhi's guests, we came to know all the manufacturers he used. It was so interesting to visit the tiny plants, miles from anywhere, and to see wooden printing blocks actually being carved, then being used to transfer their individual designs onto the various fabrics. Although a few of the dyes were imported from chemical companies (like ICI!), most were derived from vegetables or even rocks and stones which abounded in their native soil.

B advised at a very early stage of a new collection which colours, prints and styles would be most successful, and Lakhi listened. The result was a collection of advance samples, which we could show back home, resulting in even more coverage in the press and more sales for him when the clothes reached the shops.

Even as he rewarded our little business with ever-growing fees and invitations, we knew that Lakhi expected a lot in return. Nothing upset him more than to open his favourite newspaper or magazine to find one of his competitors' garments featured instead of his own. Of course, this could happen. They had PRs as well!

On trips to India, he would put us in top hotels, with no expense spared. We were of course extremely grateful, though sometimes having to put up with his irritating habits. Sometimes he would leave us stranded in a hotel lobby, waiting all morning for a car that never came, while he had forgotten us and taken off somewhere else on a completely different project. But we just loved India with all its charms and would put this down as one of them.

I remember once he invited us to a very beautiful garden party at the mansion house of one of his friends, and he introduced us all around as his British publicists. Then he suddenly turned to me and said, "Tony, come!" I followed him to his car where he produced a very early and very large video camera, which he had apparently brought to film everyone at the party. The trouble was that it was powered, at the end of a long cable, by two extremely heavy car batteries in a box, which he asked me to carry for him. So it transpired that, instead of basking in his praise and enjoying the endless champagne, I spent the whole hot afternoon following him from one group to another carrying this great box. Sometimes I would take a break and have a word with one of the interesting guests or models, only to be interrupted in mid-sentence by "Tony, come!" as the cable went tight! So it was not always a bed of roses, and sometimes I had to remind myself that nowadays I was supposed to be my own boss!

When we had known Lakhi for five years or so, he decided that he was going to introduce a range of expensive clothes specially designed for wealthy Indian women living in New Delhi and Bombay (now Mumbai). To introduce the range and display the clothes properly, he asked us to approach John Walford, even then the leading producer in the field of fashion shows. John agreed to put a show together using a dozen of London's top catwalk models, whom he would select. We all flew out, including our daughter Caroline who was to help as a dresser during the two shows, one in each city.

Our first show was in the Taj Hotel in New Delhi and I couldn't believe how many wealthy couples crowded in to see what I suppose was the first top-class professional fashion show to be staged in India. Over 300 ladies and gents in their fine silks and elaborate turbans presented a spectacle of their own as they waited for the show to begin.

All was ready offstage when Lakhi came into the wings and asked me to go out in front to introduce him, his company and the show itself. I had no warning, but that was okay – it was my job, after all. But then, just as I was stepping out, clearing my throat for the announcement, he stopped me. Inexplicably, he asked me to finish my introduction by thanking Cathay Pacific Airlines for flying us all out from London free of charge for this important event. This didn't make sense to me, because we had travelled with their arch rivals on that route, Air India, and I reminded him so. Never mind, he said, explaining that he had an arrangement with Cathay Pacific whereby, if such an announcement was made in front of all those rich people, the airline would give him six first-class tickets for him and his whole family to fly round the world!

No amount of remonstration had any effect, so towards the end of my introduction I drew a deep breath and called out: "Finally, ladies and gentlemen, I would like to thank the wonderful Cathay Pacific Airlines for flying us all out from London for this important event in supreme comfort and completely free of charge." As a few in the audience began to applaud, imagine how I felt when a particularly imposing figure, resplendent in turban, beard and gold-trimmed clothes, stood up in the third row, shouting, "So how was it that I saw you all on Air India?" Lost for words, I backed away towards the wings, proclaiming, "Let the show begin!!" I never did hear whether Lakhi got his tickets, but knowing him as I did I expect so.

After that, he paid for us all to stay for a couple of nights in, for me, the most beautiful hotel in the world, the Udaipur Lake Palace. Formerly the home of the maharaja, it seemed to float, as it rested on a low island in the middle of that mysterious lake, offering the most unimaginable luxury.

After travelling and working almost non-stop, on the first afternoon most of our twelve model girls stripped off and proceeded to sunbathe topless on the terrace. I explained to them that some of their fellow guests might take exception, but of course they carried on any way. As it turned out, the problem was not with the other guests, who didn't seem to mind at all, but I did have a complaint from the hotel manager, who said that his male staff were being distracted from their duties. This was awkward for me but eventually it was agreed that high screens made of woven grass would be erected around the terrace. The manager went off, apparently satisfied, but even that didn't work, because the male employees all suddenly found work on the second floor of the hotel where they had an even better view down!

Those girls learnt that it didn't pay to ignore my advice. I told them quite clearly that, while they were welcome before dinner to visit the colourful market in the town on the lake shore, they should definitely wear suitable clothes including dresses or skirts. Absolutely oblivious, they set off in the little ferry, wearing the skimpiest tops and shorts, only to return early, complaining that they had been forced to flee the crowded market because they felt molested and had their bottoms pinched!

That trip continued to be fraught with problems. There was not sufficient premium hotel space in Bombay, so the models and Caroline were all put in a cheap hotel down town, with poor facilities and no air conditioning. To our horror, we had a call from Caroline saying that the models had told her that they had decided to go on strike if they were not moved! The second show was to take place the very next day. There was still no alternative accommodation, and Lakhi told me, quite rightly, that he was sorry but there was nothing he could do. I had nowhere to turn, but then, to her eternal credit, Caroline herself put an end to it. She told the girls that, if they persisted, her dad (that was me!) would be in a terrible and embarrassing situation, so would they please reconsider. They listened to her, and the show took place the following evening to rapturous applause.

The troupe flew back to London from Bombay, but B, Caroline and I returned to New Delhi for a celebration dinner with all the local people who were involved in the new project. There were about twenty at the table, and we were halfway through our main course when I heard someone say "PSSSST" in my right ear. Turning around I saw a stranger bending over me, and even as I remonstrated, he said in a loud and urgent whisper, "You want buy Jaguar diamond?" and thrust a card into my hand. In a flash he was gone, and I thought no more of it till the next morning when I found the card in my pocket. Rajhiv was his name, and when I called him, he said he would be round that afternoon. He came too, not only with far and away the biggest diamond I had ever seen, but a collection of rubies and emeralds, along with two long swords with bejewelled handles and scabbards.

He explained that several maharajahs had retained him to sell off privately some of the precious stones and other items, which they had concealed when their power and most of their possessions had been taken over by the government. He never explained why he had approached me in particular that evening, but I am sure it was nothing to do with Lakhi. I was certainly not going to get involved in any actual smuggling, but being intrigued and seeing the possibility of making some lucrative introductions, I told him I would do what I could.

It so happened that, three months later, I met a man at a dinner in London, who told me he had been involved in the sale, at a high price, of a very early copy of the Koran to a collector in the Middle East. Accordingly I mentioned my Indian experience and he told me that he had other contacts who could be very interested to buy through him. When he said he would need to show photographs of the items, I explained that I had none, but would see what I could do. Then, in two short weeks, I bought myself a good Canon camera with flash and a macro lens for taking close-up pictures of small objects. Thanks to B and her two brilliant assistants, the business was fine, with no fashion week due for three months, so, having phoned Rajhiv, I got myself a return ticket to New Delhi.

While there was absolutely no connection with my last visit or that speech, the cheapest direct flight was offered by Cathay Pacific, and I settled down with a good book for the long trip. I had recently found that I needed glasses and had bought a small pair of the strength necessary for reading or any close work (like taking pictures of precious jewels!) After an excellent lunch and a glass or two of wine, I felt a bit dozy, and it was those little half-moon specs that, without thinking, I removed and laid down before falling asleep.

When I awoke, the tray had been cleared away. There was no sign of my specs, and I realised that they must have been on it. I panicked a bit, because I certainly couldn't inspect or photograph accurately all that valuable jewellery if I couldn't see it properly. To come all this way to take pictures of just the larger items Raghiv had shown me would be a waste of time and money. When I asked the nice Chinese stewardess to have a look for me, she agreed and told me not to worry, so I didn't.

The trouble was that she came back in half an hour to say that they had not been handed in and none of her colleagues had seen them either. I thanked her, but explained again that they must be on my tray. She said that there were nearly four hundred dirty trays, and she hoped that I was not expecting her to go through the whole rack into which they had been slid. "Certainly not," I said. "But could I?" Well, she got permission and I was shown to the galley where I started sliding each tray out of its slot. The process could, I thought, be speeded up a little, because I remembered leaving half of a baked potato which I couldn't face. That didn't help much, though. As I discovered, a lot of my fellow passengers had felt the same about the potato!

It took me nearly an hour, as I inspected the remains of over three hundred dinners, but then, with a yelp of joy, I found the little things, nestling half under that potato. So, after all, I arrived in New Delhi complete with all the equipment I needed to pursue my treasure hunt!

Once again Rajhiv came to my hotel, this time with even more beautiful things, including emeralds, rubies and even an exquisite pearl necklace with matching teardrop earrings. He even mentioned a vintage Rolls Royce with brackets to hold elephant guns, which was for sale. I told him that might be a bit of a problem, but proceeded with photographing everything else he brought to my bedroom over the next couple of days.

Back I went to London with the most mouth-watering pictures of priceless jewellery (but not of the car!). As I passed copies to my contact, together with price indications, I was careful to make it clear that, if he were to find buyers, he would have to be responsible for getting the jewels out of India in a legal fashion. Apart from making the introduction, I could not be involved, although, in the event of a sale, I would be entitled to a small commission.

I was dreaming. The man had professed to know personally several of the oil rich sheiks in the Middle East, who would just love to get their hands on such treasures. But he was all talk, and turned out to be a fairly well-known concert pianist with several pending overseas assignments. My excitement petered out, but it was a pity. I had begun to think it might turn into yet another little career for me.

Our connection with India Imports thrived for years until the day we closed our business. Lakhi took us or paid for us to go to the most amazing places. We stayed on a houseboat on Lake Dal in Srinigar, capital of Kashmir (there I found another treasure which I am still hoping to buy, quite legally, one day, so it has to be secret, I'm afraid). He also took us to see the Taj Mahal in Agra. That unforgettable day started off about 6am at Delhi Station with Lakhi making a fuss about the locomotive that was to haul our train. He had specifically requested one of the original steam engines for us but this one was a modern diesel and he insisted that it be changed.

That morning, the Agra train left about thirty minutes late but yes, it was hauled by a real live puffer engine. That was Lakhi for you, and we shall never forget the man. He has retired now but his business (trading under the name of Phool, which means flower) still thrives in London, run by his lovely children with all the skill and gusto that was his.

* * *

India was not the only place to which my varied job took me. France, Italy and Germany all had their exhibitions, which I attended from time to time. Organisers in New York and Dallas invited certain of my clients, whom I accompanied in the interests of publicity. We even represented a Turkish designer who took me to Istanbul for a week to see how and where his unusual clothes were made. There I enjoyed top entertainment, including a scary trip in a fast launch up the Bosphorus to the Black Sea, coming to a halt on a smooth submerged black rock on the way!

I suppose the most exciting trip was my first visit to New York City in 1977, which started in typical fashion a couple of minutes after I disembarked at Kennedy Airport. I needed some change and enquired of my porter in my best English "Is there a bank around here, please?" Turning to me with a big grin and a great Southern accent he cried out, for all to hear, "You'se in the Big Apple now, boy, we gut EVRITHIN'!"

It so happened that the exhibition being attended by our strong British contingent coincided with the grand opening of Studio 54, the most famous disco ever. Ann Chubb, who was in our party, was invited and asked me to escort her. I readily accepted and took her along to the party of all parties. Amongst the trendy New York crowd, we danced the night away to the noisiest of all noises! The new club received rapturous notices in all the papers the next morning.

But surely the most adventurous, though disastrous, trip was when one of my successful clients asked me to accompany his sales manageress Jean to Hong Kong and Tokyo on a marketing trip. It started fine, with rooms in the wonderful Mandarin Hotel. We were wined and dined in an exclusive club in Repulse Bay, and taken around Hong Kong Island the next day on a private dhow belonging to the owner of one of the island's best-known boutiques. The boat was brand new with a uniformed crew, who served us during the trip with anything we wanted to eat or drink. On our return to the hotel, I retired to my room to phone the press and arranged a very successful interview with the *South China Morning News*, which carried a good story and pictures two days later.

Then we moved on to Tokyo, where we had no stockist, but hoped that, with the right sort of publicity, we might be able to interest an agent to represent us in Japan. To this end I got on the phone, and, to my amazement, hit the bullseye first time. It wasn't easy because of the language problem, but the producer of Nippon TV's national morning news programme showed interest and accepted my invitation to dinner at our hotel that evening.

When he arrived, we took him to Jean's room to show him our range, which he really liked, saying they would be ideal for the Japanese market. By the time dinner was over, it was arranged that he would bring a model early in the morning two days later, and film Jean live, as she described the clothes, helped by an interpreter. With that, he thanked us for dinner and hurried home.

When I met Jean for breakfast, I was still delighted at the prospect of such amazing PR, but not for long, when she told me that she had made an important date in Osaka on the agreed date and had to catch the early morning bullet train. She expected me to contact the producer to postpone the appointment till her return; I did try, but in vain. He made it clear that no other dates were available, and he particularly wanted the lady sales manager to describe the dresses to his viewers. I was distraught, but nothing could be done, and that wonderful chance was lost, as I was left alone in the hotel the next morning.

As it turned out, though, that time was not entirely wasted for me. Taking a taxi (whose driver wouldn't unlock the door till I had paid!) to the big central market, I wandered for a couple of hours amongst the fascinating stalls, which offered every kind of Eastern merchandise of which I had ever heard, and more besides. Then, just as I was trying to find my way out, I spotted a little man who was selling second-hand kimonos. Flicking along one of the rails, I saw and felt their beauty, and soon realised that many of them were originals from the twenties and thirties. Seeking the assistance of the stallholder, I selected a dozen examples, all made from heavy silk and featuring the most wonderful designs, mainly in art deco. After some very tricky bargaining in pidgin English (the only Japanese word I had learnt during my short visit was *benjo* for lavatory, which wouldn't help much!), I bargained a little, giving him just under a hundred US dollars, and set off in search of the taxi rank, carrying two heavy cardboard boxes. Several of the kimonos were given away on my return to England but those we kept were to be sold, at a considerable profit, in a special little shop, which B was to open in our new life which, unknown to me at the time, lay ahead.

In the meantime, back in Tokyo, more troubles awaited me. The morning after Jean had gone off to Osaka, I rose early to take a photograph of Mount Fuji with the sun shining on it. Unfortunately, although my room was on about sixth floor, there was a large advertising hoarding on the road outside which obstructed the lower half of the mountain, as seen from my bedroom window. Accordingly I decided to nip up to the roof, from which I would be able to see the whole wonderful view through my lens.

As I got out of the lift, I saw a sign ahead, which clearly said EXIT in English lettering, so I pushed the door and found myself on the roof. The temperature, at something below zero, was a bit of a problem for me in my shirt sleeves, but there was Fujiyama in all her glory and I reckoned that a few clicks of my camera wouldn't take long. They didn't either and within a couple of minutes, I turned to get back into the warm. But no, that door had swung quietly closed behind me, and there was no handle on the outside.

At first I kept calm. The roof was the size of a football pitch with all sorts of structures, including a big restaurant, all with one or two doorways. But as I searched around, finding them all locked and deserted, panic did set in. By this time I was really cold, and as it was not yet 8am I saw no hope of anyone opening up that rooftop restaurant, where the chairs were all piled on the tables, for hours to come.

Shivering, and wondering what on earth I could do to save myself from freezing to death up there, I became desperate and went to the parapet to see whether perhaps there may be some form of fire escape. But no. Looking down, all I could see were hundreds of little black heads, a dozen floors below. Suddenly, I knew what to do. Taking a deep breath I yelled with all my might: "H-E-E-E-L-P!"

The effect was instantaneous, as all those little black heads changed colour, looking up at me. Then it seemed as if at least half of them disappeared into the hotel entrance below. At first relieved that I had obviously been heard, a minute later I was appalled at the effect of my shout, when half a dozen uniformed staff burst through that door, rushed over and grabbed me. Their apparent immediate concern was to prevent me from jumping!

Chapter Ten

Our PR business under B and her girls had thrived in my absence and this enabled me to pursue yet another opportunity, which had presented itself over the previous couple of months: special offers.

Several times, during those lunches with fashion editors of big newspapers and magazines, I had been asked whether I could help with the manufacture and dispatch of different items, which they wanted to offer their readers through their columns. The idea was that the latest dress design, or maybe a trendy skirt or a useful tracksuit, could be featured editorially, often in full colour, with descriptive copy and a coupon, which would enable readers to buy one by mail order. There would be a profit built in for the publishers, who also expected that in addition each special offer would result in more and more happy readers. The great thing was that all the space, photography and even the model were supplied by the publication itself.

After several false starts I discovered a factory in the Midlands whose owners were prepared to make up photographic samples, often overnight, and to quote reasonable prices. These would include the cost of manufacture, their own profit, postage and packing, which they themselves would also carry out and, guess what, a little percentage for me!

Of course I knew quite a bit about mail order from Biba days, and didn't hesitate to comment on the various proposals put to me. For instance, if a suggested item looked like having a fit problem or perhaps was made of a fabric that might not be instantly available in quantity, I knew it was best to say so! There was always a contract to be signed on behalf of both the supplier and the publication, which specified initial quantities to be ready in advance, and repeats guaranteed to be manufactured and despatched in no more than twenty-eight days. In the event of my people failing to supply the agreed quantities in the right quality and within the specified period, there were penalties, so the factory and I would work closely together, especially in the early sampling stages, to ensure that every eventuality could be covered. Once the offer appeared I would collect the completed coupons from the paper or magazine, and rush them to the factory. No time to waste!

The very first offer was a luxurious towelling robe, which I had sampled and costed for *The Sunday Times*. After a few weeks of adjustments and negotiations I received a call from the administrative manager of Times Newspapers, inviting me to meet him at his club one lunchtime. When I arrived, he was in the spa, wearing a sample of our robe in chocolate brown. Not for long though, as to my surprise he invited me to join him in the sauna. In there we chatted about many things other than robes or mail order until we showered and dressed. Then, over a small glass of grapefruit juice, he gave me the contract to approve on behalf of the suppliers. Having checked it through, I applied my rather sweaty signature and as soon as possible excused myself to go and find something to eat!

Four weeks later there appeared a large and rather sexy picture of a lovely girl wrapped up in my robe, styled by Brigid Keenan, the fashion editor, who wrote that she had always dreamt of sharing one like that with Clark Gable! We had 600 ready as required by the contract, across three colours and three sizes. It sold nearly 3000!

Talk about a baptism of fire! The factory and I combed the fabric showrooms all over London, the Midlands and beyond for substantial quantities of towelling. Two weeks after the huge rolls started arriving at the back door of the factory, first hundreds, then thousands of bathrobes left the front in their neat packages. It was tight, but in the end we managed. Both the colours and the thickness of the towelling did vary a bit from the original, but there were only a few returns and even fewer complaints from readers.

I made a commission of nearly 50p for each robe, and this spurred me on to develop this new wing of my small but still growing business. Over the years that followed, working with the same factory, I did every kind of special offer imaginable from Babygros in stretch towelling featured by *Mother* magazine to printed dresses in *Woman* and tracksuits in *Cosmopolitan*. Of the hundred and fifty or so offers we did, just over two thirds succeeded, with some of the others going so badly that we were left with much of the initial stock, to be sold below cost to sundry gentlemen who called at the back door of the factory. We certainly had some anxious times, but overall it was well worth doing, and I had a good deal of excitement every time a new offer broke!

Early one autumn, I sat down at lunch with the fashion editor of *The Sun* to explain to her how we operated, whereupon she asked whether we could make a suspender belt in elastic and black or white lace! Well we never had, but, undaunted as usual, the factory sent me several samples by train two days later. Based very near Nottingham, the home of lace, they had come up with some beauties that would sell at £2.25 in the paper, including postage and packing. A couple of weeks later, the fashion editor's favourite design appeared on Page 3, worn by a well-known topless model. It occupied almost the whole of a page, including the coupon and some very juicy words. We sold 34,000!

This time some people did have to wait a bit more than the promised twenty-eight days, but *The Sun* understood and they were actually pleased at the way we handled it. So pleased that, with Christmas coming up, I got a call saying they wanted to do it again, but this time in red satin!

I hardly dared phone the factory after what they had just gone through but they were brilliant as ever and put three samples in a box for me to collect from St Pancras Station's parcel office two days later. I took a taxi from there to

Bouverie Street where *The Sun*'s offices were located, and opened the box on the way to check the contents. Wrapped in tissue were three samples in red satin with black lace and elastic drops. They were just what I had envisaged and the attached prices were also attractive. It was with high hopes then that I repacked the box, paid and jumped out of the cab as it got caught in busy traffic somewhere along Fleet Street, close to my destination.

As I hurried along the crowded pavement dodging shoppers and journalists who always frequented that area, I heard the urgent blowing of a horn. As heads turned at the noise, I saw that it was coming from my taxi, which had nearly drawn level. The driver had his head out of the window, shouting to me, "Is this yours mate?" as he waved a scanty red suspender belt, which in my hurry must have slipped out of the box. As I thanked him and buried myself back in the startled crowd, my face must have been the same colour as my precious sample!

Thank goodness they didn't put it in the paper for nearly two months, so the factory was able to prepare properly. When it did appear, again on a full page, it was in full colour with a banner proclaiming, "Be a Scarlet Lady!" The price was £3.95, including postage and packing and we sold just fewer than 22,000. Again we managed and again my commission was substantial. That was when B and I finally decided that we could afford to buy our first and only brand-new yacht. Resisting the temptation to call her anything to do with suspenders we settled for *Sun + Sand*, after one of our favourite clients, who made easily the most stylish t-shirts in the world. They were pleased with the extra publicity as we sailed up and down the Solent, with their name in large capital letters clearly visible on port and starboard!

Our brand new yacht

CHAPTER ELEVEN

Quite apart from sailing, we were able to pursue our other great love – art deco. Our beautiful house in West London to which we had moved in 1978, was full of it (not quite right for a house built in 1904, but we didn't mind!), and we travelled far and wide to see exhibitions of masterpieces designed or built in the twenties and thirties.

We even went to the first World Congress of Art Deco in Miami, held in memory of Barbara Capitman, the brave lady who had lain down in front of bulldozers to save some of the wonderful buildings on South Beach there. Later, we attended another World Congress in Naples, the city in New Zealand almost entirely rebuilt in the style of art deco following a devastating earthquake in 1931.

As I approached my fiftieth birthday, I began to wonder whether it might be time for a change in our day job. B felt likewise, and we began to seek a project which would take us out of London, preferably by the sea in Devon or Cornwall, both of which we had come to love, after sailing so often into their pretty harbours and creeks. We agreed that we would start looking down there for a likely project and that, if one presented itself which incorporated a little

213

deco style, so much the better, but certainly not a condition of any sort.

Throughout the winter and spring of 1984/5 we looked and looked, making many plans. One was to create a marina in Devon's Charlestown Harbour, then to open a rooftop cocktail bar in Cornwall's Fowey, and lastly to take over a chandlery on the famous Helford River. None of these or other projects came to anything (sometimes because the premises weren't even for sale!) and, as my birthday came and went in June, we became resigned to continuing our careers in fashion, which had been so kind to us. My dream of running my own chandlery, exchanging yarns with visiting yachtsmen, perhaps over a pint of ale, as the sun sank below the horizon would remain just that, a dream.

Then it happened. In Devon, BBC Spotlight TV ran a piece about a tiny island that was for sale 200 yards off the south coast between Plymouth and Exeter. On it there were three small cottages, a fourteenth-century pub and, wait for it, an art deco hotel, built in 1929! We could hardly believe it. As I later wrote, 'A fine example of one of our best loves, surrounded by gallons of the other!' It was described as a tidal island, which became accessible by land twice a day as the tide ebbed and flowed.

That was on 20 November 1985. At 11am the day after, we met with the agent in the island's Pilchard Inn, then walked with him up to the front door of the hotel. There had been two of those doors, but one had fallen off, left to lean against the porch. This gave us an idea of what was awaiting us. The whole place had that abandoned look, with wet walls, damaged floors and botched repairs everywhere we looked. In the wonderful palm court, parts of the huge stained-glass dome had fallen and were lying on the parquet floor, shattered, amongst piles of junk and rusty scaffolding. The adjoining sun lounge had lost more than half its glass roof. Efforts had been made to fill in the gaps with plywood, but there remained big holes, through which had fallen small pebbles and salt, presumably carried there on the sea-water spray during winter storms.

The decaying palm court

The agent explained that the hotel had closed in 1955 and, for the last thirty years, had been used as self-catering flatlets for ten weeks each summer. Would we like to see the accommodation? he asked.

Following him up the uncarpeted stairs (the lift was marked 'Danger of Death – do NOT use'), we were staggered at the state of the flatlet into which he led us. There was a kitchen/dining room with a few sticks of furniture, a threadbare piece of cord carpet, stained by water which had evidently leaked through the ceiling, and a slightly rusted Baby Belling cooker on the floor in one corner. In the bedroom, there were two single beds, which hinged down from the wall for mum and dad and bunks for the kids. Between these two rooms there was a bathroom with a huge cast-iron bath, original plumbing and tiles. These were pale blue with black lines, in a typical pattern obviously created fifty years before.

There were apparently fourteen of these flatlets, of which two had been modernised by the present owners as show flats, but all the others remained in this sorry state. The necessary work, added to that which would have to be done on the ground floor, looked far too much for us, and as B and I exchanged glances in the damp bedroom, that was exactly what we were signalling to each other.

We had noticed that both rooms had rusty metal French windows, opening onto a balcony. Asking the agent to open one, we stepped out to one of the most glorious views of land and sea we could remember.

Two or three miles to the east, there was the dark shape of a headland being lashed by waves so big that, even from that distance we could watch them break. Nearer to us, a lone windsurfer was streaking out to sea, jumping the waves and ducking beneath the gulls as he went. To our right, there was an almost circular sea-water pool, about fifty yards across, surrounded by high cliffs; the agent told us that it was tidal and called the Mermaid Pool. Almost directly beneath us, stretching to the mainland, was the beach across which we had walked. As we watched the waves breaking from left and right beneath us, that strip of sand almost imperceptibly narrowed, and we began to think we had better hurry!

Turning to the agent, we said that we had better leave because of the tide. "Don't worry," he said, "you can go by sea tractor." We had seen an apparently broken-down and rusty-looking contraption parked on the beach. It didn't look too promising, but, assuming that he meant this would give us more time, we asked to see the ballroom and the restaurant. These two large areas were in the same state as everywhere else, but again we saw signs of original twenties fittings, including matching rows of wall lights and silver painted radiators two feet wide and at least eight feet high (not working though!). In the entrance hall, there hung original ceiling lights typical of the design for which we had combed London for our home. With more frequent glances behind the agent's back, our excited eyes were saying to each other: "It's fantastic, maybe we ought to have a go."

So far we had been worrying about the possibility and cost of doing all that work, but, quite apart from that, we had no idea of the price for the island itself. When I cornered the agent, he prevaricated and kept changing the subject, as the tide slowly covered the beach. After a couple of drinks in the Pilchard Inn, the driver took us all through the mounting waves to the mainland on the lurching sea tractor. On the way, the agent persuaded us to have dinner and stay the night with him and his wife. After a good deal of brandy, in the early hours of the morning, he finally told us. "Half a million pounds for the island and everything on it." I gulped on my drink and suggested to B that it was time to go to bed.

Next day, unshaven and rather the worse for wear, I settled down with B on the train to London, doing sum after sum on the notepad she had brought with her. Carefully, we laid plans as to how we could not only renovate that beautiful forgotten place, but also re-launch it in time for the forthcoming holiday season. First though, we had to buy it, and quickly too, because the agent had told us that the whole island and contents of the buildings were to be auctioned in three weeks if it remained unsold.

Armed with detailed figures, plans and the photographs we had taken, we dashed from bank to bank, seeking support for the purchase. Many, including our own, turned their backs on us, but the seventh, Allied Dunbar, agreed, as long as we put our house on the market, to lend us the full price. But the owners of the island, after thanking us for the offer, then increased the price by £50,000! Even then, we managed by deciding to sell the three little island cottages, for which we had no use. The purchase of the whole island was then speedily agreed. Two days before we were to complete, there was an auction of all the contents. Not wishing to identify ourselves, our good friends the Cherries came down from London and bought a few items on our behalf, but, having little spare cash, we had to let many go unsold. The next day, to our horror, we saw from the mainland a plume of smoke coming from the Mermaid Pool, where they were burning piles of unsold furniture which had been in the hotel since the thirties. Unable to do anything about it, we decided on an early bed in the house we had rented and on 6 January 1986, stepped from our very own sea tractor onto our very own island!

The Sea Tractor

Easter, heralding the early part of 'the season' was only three months away and we had so much to do. A freezing gale was blowing which didn't help. Everything, including the sea tractor and the giant central heating boiler needed repair, all of which was going to cost. We had some money from our precious endowment policies, the yacht and our old Daimler, but, until our London house sold, we still owed the bank nearly four hundred thousand pounds and interest rates were hovering around 16%! But it was too late to start worrying. We had done our sums. Now we had to make them work and get the show on the road!

That first evening, when everyone else had gone ashore, and the sea was raging between us and the mainland, I took B down to the Pilchard Inn. There I built a little fire in the grate and poured each of us a drink. As we drank and toasted our crazy venture, we were visited by the ghost of Tom Crocker, the island's notorious smuggler. The door, with its heavy latch, opened by itself, first the top half then the bottom. Neither of us felt like talking as it seemed that someone had joined us by the fire. He didn't stay long though, before closing the two sections of the pub's stable door *against* that strong gale. We didn't stay long either! Finishing our drinks as quickly as possible, we fled back to our hotel as fast as our legs would carry us. We had some bedding which we had brought with us, and turned in early, hoping not to dream of ghosts. Actually, Tom was friendly and although there were several stories of people being scared he never did bother us. The howling wind and a dozen slamming doors did their best that night to keep us awake, but we slept soundly till the seagulls woke us at daybreak.

During December we had assembled a group of seven lads to help us with the renovation. Between them, they knew about plumbing, electrics, carpentry, plastering and painting. They were mainly local, so they knew where to obtain the materials and tools we needed. Every minute counted if we were to be ready on time, so they all had to live on the island. Twice a day the tide came in and stayed for six hours. We couldn't have them waiting for it to part down on the beach. True, we had the sea tractor, and had employed Jimbo, its jovial Cornish driver, but the machine, driven by hydraulics, often failed to start or, worse, broke down halfway across. We couldn't risk our gang in those mighty waves, we needed them too badly!

I wish I could say it was plain sailing from then on. Not at all. Those boys were no angels. They worked hard all right, but every one of them smoked and drank hard too, and, perhaps to finance the latter, stole tools and some of the precious materials we had bought. One of the electricians bought seemingly miles of cable for re-wiring the whole place, most of it, we discovered later, three times the necessary size. The difference in cost, especially when we were on such a tight budget, was nearly fatal.

Almost daily we were hit by something totally unexpected. B had been to Plymouth and done a wonderful deal on many rolls of good strong cord carpet, and, as the west wing neared completion, we employed a man to lay it throughout the two upper floors. It was a week's work and he had nearly finished when we had a visit from the fire officer. This didn't worry me because all the alarms were installed, together with their 'break glasses' and illuminated exit signs. There were fire extinguishers in all the right places and expensive stuff called 'intumescent strip' on the doors, as required. I showed him round proudly and all was going well until, stepping over the carpet layer who was putting down the last piece at the end of a corridor, the officer said, "Just a moment." Next minute he produced a screwdriver from his pocket and levered up one of the wooden boards, which were about to be covered. Wondering what this could be about, I looked down as the board came loose to reveal STRAW! He looked up at me as I looked down at him. Then we both looked at the carpet layer, who was looking at us. We all knew what this meant: fire hazard.

That wing had been added before the war and the architect had specified strummet (compressed straw) for sound and temperature insulation. It is said that it also saved that wing from destruction, when in 1942 the blast from a high explosive bomb removed most of the original building. The straw, having been crammed, fifty years before, tightly into every corner, had dried out and half turned to dust. Not only did all the carpet have to come up but we all had to don masks and remove the wretched stuff. It burned very brightly outside and I could see what the fire officer meant! We had no time (or money) to provide alternative insulation, which, as far as I know, is still absent! With Easter fast approaching, it was more urgent to concentrate on installing brand-new Phillips kitchens in the flats and finding suitable furniture.

Friday, March 7, 1986

'Crackers' but island's new owners have the Midas touch

STORY
OF A
WHIRLWIND
ROMANCE

by Marie
Sheehy

Owners of Burgh Island, Tony and Beatrice Porter

Not sure about that!
(Reproduced by kind permission of South Hams Newspapers)

The beautiful floors in the Palm Court, sun lounge and ballroom were made of parquet, terrazzo or beech. All had suffered terribly from neglect, salt and sand and had even been deeply scratched by careless movement of scaffolding and heavy furniture. This was something we had failed to include in our costings, but by hiring the necessary machinery, abrasive compounds, and so on, we did manage and they came up shining like new. (Little did we realise how much we would pay contractors to come every week for the next fifteen years to keep them like that!)

The other things that plagued us were the 'village boys'. They lived in Bigbury-on-Sea on the mainland opposite, and for years had crossed at low tide to use the old hotel as a place to amuse themselves. Thank goodness they did not vandalise the place (well, not much), but had enjoyed themselves to such an extent that they kept coming, even after we moved in. Morning noon and night, we would find them poking their noses in everywhere. Once, one of them even crept into the room where we were staying, and B saw him. She caught him and gave him a piece of her mind. It wasn't till later that she realised that, while she was ticking him off, his discarded cigarette was burning a hole through our new carpet!

* * *

While the work continued apace, and we began to keep out the wind and rain (with a little coaxing, even the central heating began to work spasmodically), I turned my mind to marketing. We had given many undertakings to the bank, the house in London was taking ages to sell and regular interest payments had to be made from Easter onwards. This meant that we needed to attract customers to come and stay with us in this place, which although once famous, had been closed for thirty years and was now completely forgotten.

By no means everyone had a computer in 1986 and, if the World Wide Web even existed, I certainly didn't know anything about it or how to use a website for publicity. So I resorted to good old PR. British people love islands because they live on one. Then there was the art deco connection, and the huge risk we had taken, all adding up to a really good story for the press.

I found out that Agatha Christie had visited, basing two of her famous mysteries on the island. Noel Coward had come for three days and stayed for three weeks. Edward had brought Mrs Simpson on their yacht to visit and Charlie Kunz had been in residence for a whole season to entertain on the piano. Guests had danced to the music of Harry Roy and his Mayfair Four!

The story was a publicity dream, and I pressed on, preparing to mail out a press release along with new photographs. I began to imagine welcoming the travel editor of *The Times* or *Daily Telegraph* as he or she arrived on the newly painted sea tractor.

Again though, there was a problem. No matter how much press coverage might appear, with pictures to be drooled over by literally millions of readers, it was useless if we didn't have something to send them when they telephoned or wrote, expressing their interest. That meant that, in two short weeks, I had to design, write and produce a brochure and a tariff.

I used pictures of the self-catering flats (each of which by then had locally made furniture and a new kitchenette installed against the sitting-room wall), of the building, the pub and, from the mainland, of the island itself. (This latter photograph, over which I took enormous care, was actually printed in the resultant colour brochure back to front. However, because the island was so close to being equilateral on both sides, it didn't show too much, and by that time it was too late to change it anyway!) After delving further into the history, I was able to write scrumptious paragraphs about what had happened there. So, by the time

I had added the rates and the facilities we offered (fabulous cliff walks, sandy beaches, snooker, ping pong, tennis, laundry and a starter pack) my little brochure/tariff, though cheaply done, was just what I needed.

It worked. The papers loved it. Several sent journalists and featured us widely. The brochures went out to their interested readers, complete with booking form, and in came the reservations for our self-catering holidays, deposits and above all, INCOME!

* * *

That Easter (29 March 1986) we held a Grand Opening Ball. Peter Kent, his wife Noel and other friends of ours came to help and enjoy. Every flat filled up and another twenty-odd people came across the beach for the party on a freezing cold sea tractor trip. It wasn't much warmer in the building either, and I was down in the boiler room with my finger over a hole in a central heating pipe, when they arrived at the front door. Dashing up (a bit like Basil Fawlty) in my tuxedo to make them welcome, I asked one woman if I could take her fur coat. "Not bloody likely!" she replied as she cuddled it tightly around her. The cocktails, food, music and happy people dancing to the band (called Pennies from Devon) soon warmed the ballroom and, with a little speech from me, the place was well and truly re-launched after all those years.

Word spread and the media continued to write about us, using the most stunning photographs of the art deco and the island itself. That summer, we had no room to spare, and people happily brought their own supplies to be prepared and cooked on their smart new kitchen equipment.

It was all wrong though. The Palm Court, restaurant, sun lounge and ballroom were crying out to be enjoyed as they had been in the thirties. But we were only a self-catering establishment, with no kitchen or dining facilities. The ballroom was used for television and Palm Court for ping pong! We had two wonderful girls who made the beds and a receptionist but no other staff. While the income from self-catering was welcome, and even as the house in London sold at last, there was never going to be enough to pay off the bank and put right all the damage the building had suffered since it closed as a hotel back in 1955 over thirty years before.

For nearly two years we agonised over this, and wondered if we would ever be able to summon up the courage (and the money) for the big step. Then, one day, it was decided for us. Walking through the entrance hall, I was accosted by a military type who, I knew, had just checked into the Eddystone Flat (it was the nearest to the famous lighthouse of that name). He wanted to see the dinner menu, so that he could choose his wine in advance, in case it needed decanting!

What was I to say? Playing for time I asked him about his journey and where he and his wife were planning to go in the morning. But he kept on coming back to the menu and eventually, plucking up sufficient courage, I told him that he would have to cook his own dinner upstairs. I thought he would explode as I suggested to him that maybe, as his wife had made the booking, she could explain.

We didn't see either of them that evening, but they came down the next morning with their suitcases, saying they were checking out, that we were to summon the sea tractor and not even to think about giving them a bill! While I could see that it was a genuine mistake on their part, their attitude angered me as they stalked out. Only then did it dawn on me that we had reached a junction, and I knew what we must do. We had to get ourselves a decent kitchen and reopen the old building as a hotel.

B and I talked about it for the rest of the day and made an appointment to see the bank manager the next morning. "Here we are," I told him, "with people dying to spend money on decent food and wine, but we are having to turn away the very money we and the building [and the bank!] need so badly." I pressed him, saying that, if he would lend us a teeny bit more money to restore the hotel kitchen and furnish the restaurant, we would only need a few more staff and we would be on our way as a fully-fledged hotel.

It wasn't easy. When we first approached him, and he had seen that kitchen, complete with creepy crawlies, grease and a huge cauldron marked 'SOUP OF THE MONTH', he had shaken his head in disgust. Now he was very concerned about how much its complete restoration, to the satisfaction of the health and safety officer, would cost. But our tails were up and we did a deal, whereby he would lend us enough to carve off a quarter of that great room to make ourselves a small, but squeaky clean kitchen, complete with a reconditioned oven, fridge and sink. A new loan agreement would be drawn up, to include a few extra thousand pounds for furniture for the public rooms, initial staff wages. and so on. So a couple of days later, we were back in the bank to sign our lives away once more.

With our life policy gone, and no money left, I even used to joke about selling our children! Our very future was sunk in that beautiful, though still tired, place but we took this extra jump and, after thirty-three years of closure, the Burgh Island Hotel reopened.

* * *

We now produced a stylish, but not glossy, hotel brochure reminiscent of the thirties, complete with sepia photographs and drawings from the period. I sent a copy, together with a new and enthusiastic press release to all the prominent travel editors in Plymouth, Exeter, London and beyond. It worked even better than the first one. It had real class and of course, throughout its pages, I was now describing a hotel, not a self-catering joint. Before long, the most tantalizing features began to appear in the travel columns, bringing many enquiries, which more and more often led to advance bookings and substantial deposits. We were well and truly on our way, and actually began to pay back some of the bank loan.

The hotel with fourteen suites (two of which had two bedrooms) needed a great many more staff than we had required for the self-catering flats. The kitchen, housekeeping, restaurant, transport, maintenance, Pilchard Inn and reception needed, accounting for days off, holidays and the occasional 'sicky', a total of thirty. When we opened, this number of staff (for thirty-two residents!) was necessary only for the high season (July/August/September), but, as word spread, the 'shoulder months' began filling with guests too. By the time we reached the early nineties, we averaged 70% occupancy throughout the year. By that time we had also been granted a licence to conduct the civil marriage ceremony, which was a huge help.

The secret was to have a full complement of staff the week before Easter, to be chopped in half on 31 October. This we did by advertising in a free London magazine, popular with travellers as they arrived from overseas, looking for a summer job. When they enquired, we would interview them on the phone, giving them an idea of the job, the conditions and the salary, making it quite clear that the contract, which started at Easter, would end in the last week of October. In this way, on a chosen day, fourteen or so boys and girls from all over the world would arrive across the beach, with huge backpacks and often, surf boards.

Having shown them around, I would give them a little talk, issue Burgh Island T-shirts, then tell them that there were two free drinks awaiting them in the pub. This generous sounding ploy had a hidden benefit for us in so far as accommodation was concerned. In the staff house, we only had nine bedrooms, mostly doubles, and every Easter we found that, by the time those boys and girls had drunk our two free drinks and a few more, much sharing was arranged and our staff accommodation problem disappeared overnight! That way, everyone was happy.

For guests, we really did have plenty to offer. Quite apart from the lovely hotel itself, its unique location, cocktails and black tie dinner dances, there were many other things to do. After a walk round the island, they could have pints of real ale in the Pilchard Inn, or maybe a game of tennis. In the basement we had the original full-size snooker table (although we never completely got rid of the damp in that subterranean room). B even had her little shop next door to the ping-pong room. There she offered a wide selection of original art deco statuettes, tablewear and fabrics, which she had picked up wherever she went. In the early days she even sold our small selection of classic kimonos, all with the most wonderful deco designs. They fetched around £200 each, but sadly soon ran out. Repeats from Tokyo market were not possible!

I have written* in far greater detail about the amazing, hilarious and often tragic things which happened to us during those sixteen unforgettable years, and how we turned the tired hotel into a smart and thriving business.

The Great White Palace (Deerhill Books)
ISBN 0-9550727-0-0

The Palm Court restored

The most lovely people, many of them with well-known names, like Maureen Lipman, Whoopi Goldberg, Charles Dance and Dawn French, came and said how much they enjoyed themselves. We were totally hands-on, and I always made it my business to welcome every guest at the front door. There was always plenty of notice of their arrival, thanks to their phone call from the mainland requesting transport over the beach, either by sea tractor or Land Rover.

Having greeted them in a friendly, though formal, fashion, I would conduct them to their suite, while one of the lads followed with their luggage (plenty of cracks about what sort of Porter I was!), and showed them round. With all the personal contact we had during their stay, it was often on Christian name terms that I said goodbye a few days later, with kisses, of course, for the girls! We had a strict creed, which was always there in the back of our heads, that, when someone booked to stay with us, they had made a long journey and trusted us, not just with their money, but also with their time, which was irreplaceable. That was so true, as we ourselves once had occasion to remind the manager of a hotel in Malaysia. Arriving for a precious week's stay, we found that the tiles in and around the huge pool outside our room were being removed with noisy drills, meaning that we could not swim or indeed rest in the afternoon for most of our stay. Remonstrations had little effect, until, on our departure, the manager apologised saying that, once the pool was finished, we could come back for two free days. No thanks! That money and especially the time had gone for good.

Many of our guests became lasting personal friends. I remember in particular, one group of four who came regularly from Sussex. I went out of my way to advise them when I was invited to give a talk in Hove Town Hall. It was an art deco event, and I was not surprised to see them in the back row. What did surprise me though was when one of them started heckling and asking fatuous questions, which entailed a degree of embarrassment for me. When I remonstrated afterwards, he insisted it was all in fun, and we all had a good laugh.

Determined to get my own back, I was ready when they booked into the hotel again the following summer. Having arrived by sea tractor, they approached the front door, puffing slightly from walking up the drive from the beach. They didn't find my usual personal welcome, but only a locked front door with a big sign saying "GO HOME,

DAVID!" Watching his startled face from inside my little office window, I could see that I had indeed got my own back. Even now I wonder how many hoteliers know their guests well enough to risk such a prank!

In due course, we decided to employ a night porter. He was to come on duty at 11pm, patrol the grounds and take over security once the last guest had retired. It was comforting for me to know that someone other than me would be able to cope with minor incidents in the night, like a banging window, noisy staff or even a guest seeking pills for a headache. The man we chose, a big heavy chap, came with good references, and after a week's trial, we gave him a small room on the second floor where he could get some peace to sleep during the day. All went well at first and Gary, our head barman, expressed gratitude that he didn't have to lock his eighty or so bottles of spirits and mixers away every night, since they were in good hands. Actually, not quite so good. The night porter's references failed to mention his partiality to a spot of vodka. I suppose I was naïve to think we would get away with it, but as we later discovered, he was consuming considerable quantities, topping up the bottle with water in order to prevent anyone from noticing.

It all came to a head when one evening he failed to turn up for staff supper at 6pm. On sending someone to check his room, I was told that, although the door was apparently unlocked, it was impossible to open it, due to something heavy, maybe a wardrobe, having been moved against it on the inside. It wasn't a wardrobe. It was him, having fainted and fallen against the door.

Fearing for the man's very life, I telephoned the Devon Air Ambulance who arrived with their customary speed, landing their helicopter near the tennis court. When they too were unable to open the door, they decided to climb through a small window, accessed from the hotel roof. There they found him, collapsed unconscious against the door in a heavy heap. Two of the ambulance men managed to move him and to open the door. That was when they radioed their colleagues in the helicopter to bring a wheelchair up in the lift.

All this time I was alternating between the hallway and the Palm Court as guests appeared, all dressed up for their pre-dinner cocktails. By the time the empty wheelchair was put in the lift, there must have been over thirty guests seated in the palm court or chatting in the entrance hall. A few minutes later I saw from the indicator lights that the lift was on its way down; when it arrived, I opened the door to find this large body strapped into the chair, with its head falling to one side.

Suddenly, I knew what to do. Almost slamming the lift door, I marched smartly through the crowded hall towards the busy Palm Court shouting: "Quick – dolphins in the bay!" It worked a treat, as every single person stopped chatting and followed me, like some sort of Pied Piper, to the wide windows that overlooked the sea. As I pointed at the non-existent dolphins, I could see out of the corner of my eye two uniformed men wheeling the chair out through the front door and down the drive. A little later we heard the clatter of helicopter blades, as our guests ordered their favourite cocktails, maybe a White Lady or even an Arlene's Revenge. We never employed a night porter again, but I did hear that our only one recovered; weeks later we forwarded his little suitcase, complete with his few belongings, to an address in Cornwall.

Quite often, we were approached by photographers who wanted to use the restored hotel as a backdrop, usually for fashion magazines or newspapers. We were entitled to a location fee, and it was good for publicity. I was particularly glad when a German photographer booked for himself, his wife and four others to stay for a five-day shoot. I got to know him really well as he went about his work, using a tall and very beautiful model who came with the party.

After four days, he declared that he had finished early, and everyone could have the day off to enjoy the hotel and beach. Halfway through that busy morning, I felt the need to go to the gents, just across the lobby from my office. In a hurry, I pushed hard on the door and entered, to be met by the most extraordinary sight. There, casually leaning on one of the original 1930s urinals was that lovely girl, wearing only a pair of high-heeled shoes, and smoking a cigarette in a long ivory holder.

"Oh" I said "So sorry. Please excuse me", and retreated in embarrassment, as only an Englishman could do.

Later, telling the photographer what I had seen, he said that, if I had gone in a little further, I would have seen him round the corner in one of the cubicles with his camera.

236

"You rotter," I said. "If you don't promise to send me a copy, I'll tell your wife of you!"

Well, he did send me a large black-and-white print, which B framed. It was not at all crude, and we decided the best place to hang it would be right there in the gents, where it had been taken.

Over the ensuing weeks of that summer the picture did cause just a few comments, but then, one evening, when we had a party of Hooray Henrys from Salcombe in for dinner, I heard a particularly loud laugh coming from the gents. I thought nothing of it till much later, when I found the broken frame on the floor, minus the picture.

Fortunately I had written to thank the photographer profusely, so when I told him what had happened, he sent me another, which B also framed and hung in my private dressing room. I still have it, and the photographer's wife is none the wiser. Sorry, gents, but I have been persuaded not to include it in this book!

* * *

Throughout our time there, we always ran the hotel in a very personal way. Being new to the business and, well aware of the shortcomings of the old building, not to mention the well-meaning but often inexperienced staff, it was the only way. If a problem arose, B or I were the first to know about it and therefore best suited to solve it. But it took its toll on us. Our precious Tuesday off seldom started till lunchtime, and, even then, we often had to wait for a big rough tide to ebb before we could get away safely by sea tractor to spend the night in someone else's hotel. Quite apart from the welcome break, we often picked up tips on how a hotel should or should not be run.

Accordingly, when in the spring of 2001 a couple who had just been married on the island, asked us to sell it to them, we agreed to meet to discuss it. They seemed suitable people to whom we could entrust our 'dream' after fifteen years. A professional couple, who claimed to love the period as much as we did, they were prepared to exchange contracts on 1 May and complete the purchase on 1 October, fully five months later. They promised that our staff, many of whom had become friends, had a future with them. They also assured us that our connection with the place to which we had given so much of our lives would continue. We could bring the grandchildren to swim in the Mermaid Pool; we could also play tennis and snooker, and of course use the pub and restaurant. Although we declined, they even offered to name a suite after us! We agreed everything else and proceeded with the legalities. During one meeting at the solicitors, they even made it clear that they were so anxious to proceed that they would waive their right to a survey of the building.

It was a great summer. We were able to entertain our guests one more time and to explain to them that we had decided to move on. We spent a lot of time and money to ensure that we would leave the place in good shape for the new owners. We had agreed to spend time with them, to show them where everything was and how it all worked. However, in the event, we saw very little of them, apart from a couple of weeks during which they installed a selection of computers.

At 1pm on the appointed day, both solicitors phoned to report completion of the sale. I took champagne across the Palm Court to wish the new owners luck and to toast Burgh Island together. To my surprise, they declined, apparently preferring to drink with a friend they had brought with them. I was more concerned for Emma, our brilliant secretary, who was sitting with us and inclined to be tearful, so B and I stayed with her till she was told by her new bosses to go back to work.

Just then, out of a clear blue sky, there came a downpour, accompanied by lightning and a crash of thunder. It lasted less than a minute and the sky cleared to blue again as we all looked at each other in astonishment. What kind of sign was this! Tom Crocker saying goodbye? There wasn't time to think about it, because the heavy rain had found its way through the stained-glass dome and was dripping into the woman owner's glass!

This was not quite how we had imagined spending our last few minutes after so many years. All we could do was to try to smile our way through the farewell planned outside the front door by our faithful staff, board the sea tractor, and get away as quickly as possible (at 4 mph!)

A sad farewell

CHAPTER TWELVE

Before long we put our roots down again, this time in what we are proud to call the only art deco barn in Devon. All the rooms are furnished in our favourite style, while the walls are covered with pictures and wall vases from the period. Now, surrounded by tall trees, we swim before breakfast all year long in our warm freshwater pool rather than the chilly Mermaid one; we are woken in the morning by rooks and pigeons instead of seagulls and waves. Our new home is only fifteen minutes from Burgh Island and, although for some reason we are banned from the pub or the hotel or using the sea tractor, we are happy to wade through the water, so that we can walk round 'our' beloved island and assure her that she is not forgotten.

Having found and furnished our new home, our first act was to celebrate our 'retirement' with the family, so we took the whole lot of them for a fortnight to a hotel on Crete, especially chosen to suit all ages. On our return I shut myself away to write in detail our incredible story in *The Great White Palace* which was published in 2002. Now I was an author!

Our daughter Caroline had bought a sweet cottage in the same parish, together with her Peter and two little ones,

Oscar and Ella, who attended the local preschool. While very well run, this establishment fell short, operating as it did only four days a week in the village memorial hall, which made it very awkward for working mums. Before we moved into our house, Caroline had assembled a committee, dedicated to buying a piece of land and to building a new preschool, to be open all five working days. Before I knew it, she had co-opted me into becoming a trustee, a position to which I gave an increasing amount of time, not least in the form of fundraising.

I still had time to travel to many exotic destinations with B. We toured Mexico, Malaysia, Oman and Morocco (this last was such an amazing experience that, on our way back, I wrote to the king, congratulating him on his country and its people. I never did get a reply!). We even flew to northeast India, where we boarded a converted ferryboat on the Bramaputra river. The tour was entitled 'Tigers and Temples', but it didn't turn out like that. Admittedly, we did see a few small tumbledown temples, but nothing like what we had seen in, say, Mexico. As for tigers, not one! At a certain place we were taken, mounted astride elephants, to seek tigers in the long grass. Afterwards, while recovering from the pain of having my legs forced apart by that great neck for nearly an hour, I put a question to our guide. "When did you last see a tiger here?" to which he said, "Never, sir, but my father saw a big one over there in 1953!"

Still suffering, I hobbled over to photograph a baby elephant, whose back was about level with my hips.

Before lining up to take a picture, I gave him a friendly pat on the flank. This turned out to be a mistake. Seemingly without any effort whatsoever, he gave me a flick with his backside, sending me and my camera flying across the road into a ditch the other side. That was one picture I never did take!

Back in England, I took up golf at the Bigbury Course where I always looked forward to the fantastic views, looking down on the Island, from the sixteenth hole. Occasionally I mixed travel and golf, playing with my old friend Bruce across the Channel in Brittany.

On one such occasion we stayed in a *longere* (long house), so located that it was within easy reach of several golf courses. We liked it very much and I became interested to discover that there was a selection of ancient stone farm buildings for sale in the area, crying out for renovation. Sensing the chance of another project and a second home for the family, I flashed a picture of a terrace of three centuries-old farm cottages back to B from my mobile phone. She replied, urging me to buy them, and by the time I saw her again, my offer had been accepted, so we embarked on two years of serious renovation. It involved knocking through stone walls half a metre thick on both floors (but there were no stairs till we made some), to link the cottages together, repairing the slate roofs. Thus we created the most wonderfully comfortable living space, where, hundreds of years before, farm hands and animals had bedded down together! Having installed the handmade staircase, lined with oak, we then created three large bedrooms, each with its own en suite bathroom. Everywhere we retained the sturdy old beams, which had to be treated against years of little worms and various types of beetles!

The completed *longere* stood in three thousand square metres of fertile land, half of which I converted to a smooth grass football pitch, complete with goal, for the grandchildren to practice and keep fit. Only a couple of hundred yards away, down a steep hill, there was a local beauty spot, where ancient stepping-stones crossed a fast-flowing river. The local council was even in the process of restoring the old water wheel, which used to provide flour for a stone-built oven, twenty metres away. The work was being carried out by people condemned to community service. They were getting on fine, and it was beginning to look as if soon we wouldn't have far to go to buy fresh, warm baguettes for breakfast!

So there I was, supposed to be retired, playing the odd round of golf, enjoying my newspaper in the morning and several holidays a year, but getting busier than ever. I spent more and more time marketing my first book, through my website and carefully chosen stockists. I also applied to the south-west's head offices of the Women's Institute and other local organisations, asking if I could be put on their speaker lists. I received approval, and a few months later, when the new lists were published, the phone started to ring. I was invited by branches all over Devon to give my illustrated talk, entitled 'The Restoration of Burgh Island and its Art Deco Hotel'.

I was allowed forty-five minutes, including a short slide show, and my efforts were well received. Occasionally, though, I would spot someone asleep when I was only halfway through. Whenever this happened, I had a way of introducing a certain anecdote, during which I told of a hotel guest knocking on the reception desk to try to get attention. That was my excuse for knocking a little loudly on the table, thus awakening the offender, who then listened to the second half of my talk. None of them complained. In fact one lady actually thanked me, because she had been chosen to write about my talk in the local newspaper!

After the traditional vote of thanks, I was always permitted to sign and sell copies of my book. In this way, I met many interesting members who had questions or stories about the hotel's past. Then I enjoyed the tea and cakes, before judging a competition, usually choosing the best and most interesting of art deco designs submitted by members. It was a bit like the *Antiques Road Show*, but I wasn't expected to value them!

It was rewarding in many ways, but the timing was awkward. I was usually invited to start about 7.30 in the evening. This meant loading up my projector and screen by 6pm or so and driving, sometimes for an hour or more, sometimes to places high up on Dartmoor. On a dark winter's night, I began to find this too much, especially when I arrived home at 11pm, to crawl into bed beside my sleeping wife! Mind you, there was always something warm, waiting for me in the oven.

After two years and 115 talks, including some to Rotary and Probus Clubs, I decided to call it a day. Although my resignation was accepted and my name removed from the list, it took months before invitations dried up. After that, I was able to relax a bit in the evenings and accept dinner invitations from friends, without clashing with one of those dates.

The French project continued apace with monthly ferry trips across the Channel. The idea was to check on the work and to push the builders a bit, but this didn't really help, because, if we were there for two to four days, they would push off somewhere else, so that we could enjoy our holiday!

Back home, there was more work to do on the preschool project. Our grandchildren grew and moved onto higher schools, but Caroline kept going, as sufficient funding was raised to buy the land and to get planning permission for the new building from the local council. After a while, though, even she handed over to others and I was happy to find myself committed for years to come, although there was no longer any family connection.

As the committee struggled valiantly, completing the many long forms necessary for major fundraising applications, members did their best with raffles and coffee mornings. At one evening meeting I couldn't resist pointing out how long it was going to take to raise enough money to build a whole new preschool. Asked if I had any better ideas, I said, "How about a classic car show?" I still had my old black Citroën and noticed how heads turned when I drove by, and knew that, from time to time, rallies were arranged, which people paid to go and see.

Again, I had no idea what I had let myself in for, but, at the age of seventy-two, so began another little career. Using the few contacts I had, and contacting the various car clubs through the internet, I found considerable interest on the part of car owners, and the local council offered the village playing fields as a venue, free of charge, for our charity. I thoroughly enjoyed polishing up my old PR skills, using press and radio throughout the area, while B designed posters and leaflets. These were distributed far and wide throughout the summer of 2007, in time for the event which took place on the August bank holiday Monday.

A wide assortment of sixty-five old cars were booked in, and 950 people came through the gate. Our grandchildren were amongst the volunteers and a dozen stalls, including several selling unusual foods, gave us a share of their takings. After all expenses, our total profit was an unbelievable £3,250, a welcome contribution towards what the preschool needed. The following year, we did it again with even better results.

As the proceeds began to pile up, more substantial funding was achieved from Devon County Council, who were happy to help a group who showed that they were making big efforts to help themselves. Building commenced and the brand new preschool, complete with solar driven central heating and air conditioning opened in the spring of 2010. The youngest members of the community should be alright now, with a smart eco-friendly building (vintage car owners are offered a conducted tour) but they will still need annual running expenses, books and equipment, so it looks like I am stuck with a job for life!

All the time we had been breathing life into the hotel on Burgh Island, we had kept hearing sad tales about another art deco hotel that had fallen on hard times. The Midland Hotel in Morecambe Bay had been designed by the famous modernist architect Oliver Hill for the London Midland and Scottish Railway. They opened it in 1935 as a staging post for passengers who may have wanted to break their journey, or to visit the Lake District, whose peaks could be seen clearly across the bay. Dramatically curved with views straight out over the sea, the hotel boasted the most extraordinary features throughout, several of them contributed by Eric Gill, whose sculptures made him one of the most famous artists of the twentieth century.

After a well-publicised opening, The Midland had been *the* place to stay, but, after being used as a hospital during the war, it never regained its grandeur, and, by the time I was approached for advice by the man who owned it in the eighties, it was in a sorry state. After a series of unsuccessful efforts, a group of deco lovers, mainly from the Lancashire area, formed The Friends of the Midland, who were dedicated to the salvation of their wonderful building, by then verging on ruin. Though I was at the other end of the country, I joined like a shot.

There was not a lot I could do from such a distance, but I did attend the Annual General Meetings, in the hope that, if a developer, interested in saving this jewel, was found, I would be able to help with the PR and marketing in much the same way as I had on Burgh Island. In 2003, just such a company, called Urban Splash, did buy the Midland and set about restoring it in the most determined and thorough way. No botch job here. These people knew what they were doing, ensuring that the millions of pounds and over five years they lavished on it would never be wasted.

Six months before the opening in 2008, I made a special trip, in order to meet the director concerned, but it came to nothing, it being obvious that they had made other arrangements for the marketing of their beautiful hotel. B and I went to the opening though, and we are thrilled to read of the way in which it is thriving to this day.

Our Aveton Gifford Classic Car Shows are now famous and (except when it rains!) attracting a hundred beautiful cars every August bank holiday. The preschool is thriving and supplying a steady stream of pupils to our growing primary school. Our grandchildren are making their names in German, IT, music, and acting, with ten-year-old Susie already making great strides. Even as we watch their progress, we love to think back over the years and the funny things they said and did.

One evening, about five years after we sold Burgh Island, I was reading the paper by the fire and puffing my pipe.

Gemma, nine at the time, said to me, "Bapum, why do you smoke that pipe?"

"I started years ago. It helped me give up cigarettes."

"Why do you smoke it?"

"It relaxes me. It's only once a day, and I don't inhale the smoke."

"Do you think you'll ever give it up?"

"I shouldn't think so. It doesn't do me any harm."

Long silence… then:

"Actually, I suppose it's too late anyway now, isn't it"

She went home to London the next day, but that evening I put all my pipes in the fire, together with tobacco, pipe cleaners and other smoker's paraphernalia. Next morning there remained only a single silver ring off my most expensive pipe. Thanks, Gemma. I mean it. So does Granny B!

We always looked forward to their visits (still do), which were arranged in plenty of time. But once I was surprised to receive, only a few days before they were due, an email from Hannah, (about ten) with an attachment, saying would I make one of these before she arrived. I opened it, to find drawings describing how to make a go- cart!

Never having been very clever with my hands, but eager to please, I cannibalised an old pushchair from the shed. In the short time available, with the aid of a piece of plywood, some screws and a short piece of rope, I had it ready on time. I even painted it green and gave it a number HAN 1. It was well worth it to see the look on her face, and it still gives children, and a few grown-ups, enormous fun down our sloping lawn.

There was a time when I needed to deliver some books to Collaton Fishacre a nearby 1930s house, owned by the National Trust. It was half-term and Caroline asked if we could have Oscar, eight, and a friend for the day, so we took them with us. B and I knew that art deco house and its garden really well, but when we were invited to take the boys round, we accepted gratefully.

Over the next hour or so we took them round the various rooms, in each one of which we were welcomed by an elderly volunteer, who described the history and the contents for the boys who seemed to show at least some polite interest. Afterwards we took them home and dropped them off at Caroline's as arranged.

Later, she phoned to thank us for looking after them, and I noticed that she had the giggles. I asked what was so funny, and she told me that, on being asked where we had taken them for the day, Oscar had said, "O I don't know, some old peoples' home!"

Little Susie was only three when our Julia decided to give her a lesson on gardening and how things grow. She took her out to the front of their house with a small spade, a bucket of water and a single sunflower seed. Showing her how to plant it, she told her daughter how it would grow as long as it was watered. Susie never forgot and it grew to over fifteen feet!

Caroline's Ella was only three in the year 2000, when we still lived on the island. In the summer of that year, there was great excitement as the solar eclipse approached. We let it be known that the public would be welcome, and, on the big day our family joined hundreds of others, as we climbed to the summit. Although it was partially spoiled by a cloudy sky, we were able to see the shadow start to cover the sun, and, as it got darker and darker, it was amazing to look back at the mainland at the almost continuous line of flashes from a thousand cameras. When, as the light improved, and we could see the land clearly again, little Ella noticed the difference and I heard her say, "Mummy, can we have that again please?"

As I write, it is now 2015, and I have just celebrated a really big birthday, with wonderful caterers and a big marquee in the garden. Forty people were there, including most people in this book and more besides. Peter Kent gave a flattering speech, to which I replied by flitting through my many careers, short and long, with anecdotes thrown in to make them laugh. Then we cut the cake that Julia had made in the perfect shape of a classic Citroën. After that we had a toast, and I thought it was time to relax.

But no. Five minutes later, I was cornered by a couple of old friends in the entertainment industry, who sat me down to say how much they would like to suggest making a film about my life. "Oh no," I said. "Whatever next?"

꙰